HELL
TO PAY

HELL
TO PAY

How the Suppression of Wages
Is Destroying America

MICHAEL LIND

PORTFOLIO | PENGUIN

Portfolio / Penguin
An imprint of Penguin Random House LLC
penguinrandomhouse.com

Most Portfolio books are available at a discount when purchased in quantity for sales promotions or corporate use. Special editions, which include personalized covers, excerpts, and corporate imprints, can be created when purchased in large quantities. For more information, please call (212) 572-2232 or e-mail specialmarkets@penguinrandomhouse.com. Your local bookstore can also assist with discounted bulk purchases using the Penguin Random House corporate Business-to-Business program. For assistance in locating a participating retailer, e-mail B2B@penguinrandomhouse.com.

Library of Congress record available at https://lccn.loc.gov/2022054218

ISBN 9780593421253 (hardcover)
ISBN 9780593421260 (ebook)

Printed in the United States of America
1st Printing

BOOK DESIGN BY ALISSA ROSE THEODOR

This book is dedicated to the memory of Sherle R. Schwenninger.

Ostensibly the demand for cheap labor is made in the interest of improvement and general civilization. It tells of increased wealth and of marvellous transformations of the old and the worthless into the new and valuable. It speaks of increased travelling facilities and larger commercial relations; of long lines of railway graded, and meandering canals constructed; of splendid cities built, and flourishing towns multiplied; of rich mines developed, and useful metals made abundant; of capacious ships on every sea abroad, and of amply cultivated fields at home; in a word, it speaks of national prosperity, greatness, and happiness. Alas! however, this is but the outside of the cup and the platter—the beautiful marble without, with its dead men's bones within.

Cheap Labor, is a phrase that has no cheering music for the masses. Those who demand it, and seek to acquire it, have but little sympathy with common humanity. It is the cry of the few against the many. When we inquire who are the men that are continually vociferating for cheap labor, we find not the poor, the simple, and the lowly; not the class who dig and toil for their daily bread; not the landless, feeble, and defenseless portion of society, but the rich and powerful, the crafty and scheming, those who live by the sweat of other men's faces, and who have no intention of cheapening labor by adding themselves to the laboring forces of society.

—FREDERICK DOUGLASS, "CHEAP LABOR,"
NEW NATIONAL ERA, AUGUST 17, 1871

Power is the flower of organization.

—A. PHILIP RANDOLPH

CONTENTS

FOREWORD   *xiii*

CHAPTER ONE

The Big Lie: *You Are Paid What You Deserve*   *1*

CHAPTER TWO

The Bad End of the Bargain: *How Organized Labor
in the Private Sector Was Destroyed*   *13*

CHAPTER THREE

Boss Rule: *How Employment Practices
Are Rigged Against Workers*   *23*

CHAPTER FOUR

Global Labor Arbitrage I: *How Employers
Use Offshoring to Crush Worker Power*   *33*

CHAPTER FIVE

Global Labor Arbitrage II: *How Employers Exploit
Immigrants to Weaken Worker Power*   *45*

CHAPTER SIX

Scrooge Revisited: *The Anti-worker Welfare State*   *65*

CHAPTER SEVEN

The Credential Arms Race   *83*

CHAPTER EIGHT

Cascade Effect: *How Bad Jobs and the Credential Arms Race Make Every Social Crisis Worse*   *95*

CHAPTER NINE

The Myths of Neoliberal Globalization   *113*

CHAPTER TEN

Beyond Global Arbitrage: *Trade, Immigration, and the Next American System*   *125*

CHAPTER ELEVEN

How to Restore Worker Power in America   *145*

CHAPTER TWELVE

"Keep Your Government Hands Off My Medicare": *Social Insurance and the Work Ethic*   *165*

AFTERWORD   *181*

ACKNOWLEDGMENTS   *191*

NOTES   *193*

FOREWORD

What do falling fertility in the United States, a plague of loneliness and lack of friendship, bitter conflicts over racial and gender identity, and a politics of culture wars and moral panics have to do with one another? Like cracks in a building that radiate up from a crumbling foundation, these dystopian trends are influenced, directly or indirectly, by an underlying factor: the existence of too many bad, low-wage jobs in America.

A building's foundation can erode for a long time before an earthquake or a fire exposes the extent of the structural decay. In the same way, a series of external shocks—the Great Recession, the COVID-19 pandemic and the economic contraction it produced, and the surging inflation caused by the economy's reopening and the war in Ukraine—have illustrated rifts within American society with more fundamental causes.

Today's American crisis is the confluence of five crises: a demographic crisis, a social crisis, an identity crisis, a political crisis, and an economic crisis that aggravates the other four. The demographic crisis is one shared with many industrial societies and some developing nations: the collapse of family formation and birthrates. The social crisis is the growth of personal isolation, manifest in everything from declining numbers of friends to the withering away of membership organizations and communal institutions. The identity crisis involves the weaponization of identity politics in the zero-sum battle for jobs and status. And the political crisis has arisen from the replacement of the transactional politics of the past with culture wars on the right and moral panics on the left.

All four of these crises are worsened if not caused by the fifth, an underlying economic crisis; that is the argument of this book. The economic crisis is the existence of too many jobs with low wages, no benefits, and bad conditions in present-day America.

America's bipartisan elite has its own preferred solution to the problem of too many low-paying jobs: "Learn to code!" That trite phrase became a bitter joke during the Great Recession of the 2010s. For a generation, journalists and opinion columnists at elite media outlets, informed by the conventional wisdom among academic economists, had condescendingly told laid-off automobile workers in the Midwest and other struggling American workers that instead of complaining that their jobs had been offshored to low-wage workers in Mexico or China, they should move to Silicon Valley and "learn to code." As waves of layoffs swept through the media industry, journalists who announced on their personal Twitter accounts that they had lost their jobs found themselves mocked by critics who told them, "Learn to code!"

The learn-to-code cliché persists because it is shorthand for the dominant way that America's elite thinks about work and wages in the United States. According to the simpleminded version of economics that is all that most policy makers and pundits know, in the private sector the labor market automatically sets the wages of all workers depending on their productivity, which in turn depends on their skills. Hedge fund managers and corporate executives who earn a million times more than janitors have skills that are valued by impersonal, competitive markets vastly more than are janitorial skills.

This is a myth. It could be called a lie, if it were not for the fact that its beneficiaries, including those hedge fund managers and corporate executives, devoutly believe this theory that happens to justify their high incomes. The truth is less flattering to the economic elite: society would collapse if all low-paid workers in health care, retail, waste management, and service industries "upskilled" for jobs in the knowledge industry. In reality, wages are determined largely by the relative bargaining power of workers and employers. And right now, that bargaining power is at an all-time low.

Worker bargaining power in the United States did not die because of globalization or technological innovation. American worker power was murdered by American business and its allies among American politicians and policy makers.

The strategy of American business, encouraged by neoliberal Democrats and libertarian conservative Republicans alike since the 1970s, has been to lower labor costs in the United States, not by substituting laborsaving technology for workers, but by schemes of labor arbitrage: offshoring jobs in some sectors when possible to poorly paid workers in other countries and substituting unskilled immigrants willing to work for low wages in other sectors, like meatpacking, construction, farm labor, and commercial and residential cleaning. American business has also driven down wages by smashing unions in the private sector, which now have fewer members—a little more than 6 percent of the private sector workforce—than they did under Herbert Hoover. Another wage-suppressing tactic of American business is replacing full-time employees with benefits with part-time contractors or gig workers with lower wages and no benefits.

The result of de-unionization, offshoring of industry, and mass low-wage immigration has been the growth in the United States of a category of workers known as the "working poor," who are paid too little to survive without dependence on means-tested public assistance or "welfare" programs like food stamps and housing vouchers. Perversely, these welfare programs—including the earned income tax credit (EITC), a wage subsidy for the working poor—indirectly encourage employers in sweatshop sectors like retail to pay low wages. Why not pay low wages, as long as the taxpayers guarantee that low-wage workers and their children will not starve?

This explains why the United States, which has lost much of its manufacturing to China and other countries, remains a world leader in one area—creating bad jobs with low wages and inadequate hours and no union representation. Since the 1960s, as a share of private sector, nonsupervisory jobs, goods-producing jobs that once provided steady jobs at good wages have shrunk from 42 percent to 17 percent. Their share of the private sector workforce has been replaced almost exactly by job growth in service sectors with bad jobs and low wages: retail, leisure and hospitality, administrative, waste management, and health care and social assistance services.[1] The low wages and poor working conditions of these jobs can be directly traced back to the decimation of unions by big business.

Most of the jobs that the U.S. economy has created for the past few decades have paid poorly. That isn't going to change soon. According to the Bureau of Labor Statistics (BLS), the three jobs with the most projected growth in numbers between now and 2029 are "home health and personal care aides" ($25,280 a year), fast-food and counter workers ($22,740), and "cooks, restaurant" ($27,790). Of the twelve occupations in the United States that the BLS projects will have the greatest numerical growth in workers over the next decade, only four pay more than around $29,000 a year.[2] In 2019, the official poverty threshold for a family of four was $25,750.[3]

The growth of service sector jobs in an advanced industrial economy is not a problem in itself. The problem is that in many of these occupations, wages are so low that full-time workers rely on means-tested public assistance in order that they and their families can survive. According to a 2019 study for the Brookings Institution that defined the low-wage workforce as those who made less than $16.03 an hour, adjusted for regional differences, 26 percent of low-wage workers found themselves forced to rely on the government safety net for assistance, compared with only 8 percent of the U.S. workforce as a whole.[4]

If the effects of low wages and bad jobs were limited to the working poor, that would be a national disgrace and a challenge for social reform but not necessarily a society-wide catastrophe. But the effects of having a substantial number of workers who can never earn enough to survive without government assistance ramify throughout all of American society.

Fear of joining the miserable proles who must supplement their inadequate wages with food stamps and housing vouchers and the EITC leads more and more Americans to engage in a self-defeating credential arms race. While the wage premium associated with union membership has vanished along with unions in most of the private sector, credentials—in the form of college diplomas or occupational licenses—can act as tickets to good jobs in cartelized professions and crafts or in big, hierarchical firms that are somewhat immunized from competition by their own market power. Thanks to the desperate scramble for credentials by Americans who fear sinking into the quagmire of working poverty, licensing requirements in one trade after another have increased. And the number of Americans aged twenty-five years or older with bachelor's degrees or higher has undergone a cancerous growth from 8 percent in 1960 to 36 percent in 2020.[5]

Thanks to credential inflation, the value of diplomas declines over time. Today many college graduates find themselves working in jobs that require only a high school education or less, like the proverbial Starbucks coffeehouse worker with a bachelor's degree. As the BA becomes the new high school diploma, the master's degree becomes the new BA. In a destructive and wasteful competition for access to a limited number of good jobs, American students spend more years and more money on campus pursuing credentials whose value constantly declines.

The credential arms race, in turn, contributes to the four concurrent crises of the American regime today: the demographic crisis, the social crisis, the identity crisis, and the political crisis.[6] From our polarized elite-dominated politics to the multiplication of "identity credentials" deployed by Americans desperately competing for scarce university openings and good jobs, from the social isolation of non-union low-wage workers to the collapse of fertility caused by postponement of marriage and family life during prolonged quests for diplomas, many of the pathologies of present-day America can be traced, directly or indirectly, to the crushing by employers of the bargaining power of the American working class, the consequent proliferation of bad, low-wage jobs, and the credential arms race that has resulted.

In this book, I show how both businesses and policy makers

acting on behalf of employer interests have weakened the bargaining power of American workers by using a range of instruments: domestic labor laws that favor employers, global labor arbitrage in the form of pro-employer offshoring, and immigration policies.

I then show how America's anti-worker, pro-employer welfare state enables the growth of jobs that pay too little to live on. I discuss how the fear of being trapped in the insecure working class created by the half-century neoliberal employer offensive leads many desperate young Americans to try to replace the former wage supports of national protectionism and union membership with new forms of economic protection—college diplomas and occupational licenses. I argue that the competition of too many people for too few good jobs contributes to a number of seemingly unrelated social pathologies, from delayed or failed marriages and non-marriage to the decline of civic associations and the rise of identity politics and political polarization.

In the conclusion of this book, I sketch out what American trade, immigration, labor, and benefits policies should be if the goal is to increase the power of American workers in negotiations with employers instead of to annihilate it. In our era of increasing great-power competition and national rivalries for shares of the global market, the 1990s consensus in favor of free-market globalization is being superseded by a new understanding of the importance of government-business collaboration in national industrial policy and technological innovation. Organized labor, in new and effective forms, should take part in a new tripartite government-industry-labor partnership for production and shared prosperity.

The economist Herbert Stein is famous for what is arguably the only generalization of social science that is a universal law: "If something cannot go on forever, it stops." Having caused growing cracks to appear throughout the crumbling edifice of American society, the fifty-year war on American worker power must be brought to an end.

HELL
TO PAY

CHAPTER ONE

The Big Lie

You Are Paid What You Deserve

In 2011, the journalist Ron Suskind quoted Larry Summers, one of the leading neoliberal economists and policy makers of the last generation, as saying, "One of the reasons that inequality has probably gone up in our society is that people are being treated closer to the way that they're supposed to be treated."[1]

Outrageous as this remark seems, Summers was merely stating the conventional wisdom of academic economics, which is endlessly repeated by policy makers, pundits, journalists, business executives, and career counselors. This is the theory that wages directly reflect the actual contribution of each worker to the enterprise, from the janitor to the CEO. And this is the theory that underlies claims that government can and should do nothing to boost wages for workers, other than helping them acquire skills that the perfectly competitive labor market automatically will reward. If it is true, then rapid increases in the skills of the economic elite must explain why, in the last forty years, the earnings from labor income of those of the 95th percentile of American workers increased by 63.2 percent, while the hourly wages of the 50th percentile went up only 15.1 percent and wages of the 10th percentile only 3.3 percent.

This theory is false, even if the bipartisan establishment believes it. Obviously there is some relationship between skills and pay. But in most companies, government agencies, and nonprofit organizations, there is considerable flexibility when it comes to compensation. What workers are paid, along with their working conditions and benefits, depends on the relative bargaining power of workers and employers. Naturally workers want to increase their bargaining power, while self-interested employers want to diminish the bargaining power of their employees. The greatest hoax of our time is the success of employers in persuading the American public—and many American workers themselves—that bargaining power has nothing to do with pay.[2]

There are two ways of explaining the increasing dispersion of wages in the U.S. job market: the worker power story and the human capital story. The human capital story is the one you probably heard from your economics professor and from mainstream economists, pundits, and politicians.

The human capital story says that every individual worker's wages are determined automatically and without human interference by the worker's contribution to the output of the firm or agency. The worker's economic contribution to the firm in turn more or less directly reflects the worker's personal skills or "human capital." The lowest-paying jobs? They pay poorly because they are not providing what is most valuable as a result of advanced information technology, or global markets, or some other impersonal, irresistible force.

According to the human capital story, the polarization of wages in the twenty-first-century United States accurately reflects the skills demanded by the new, globalized, high-tech economy. Automation and other kinds of technological progress have eliminated many "middle-skilled" jobs in manufacturing. What remain are high-skilled jobs in the high-tech "knowledge economy" and low-skilled jobs in "high-touch" sectors such as low-end nursing, leisure and hospitality, and retail.[3] The human capital story is based on an academic economic theory. The marginal revenue product (MRP) theory holds that what each individual worker at a firm earns exactly reflects that individual worker's contribution to the firm's profits—not a penny more, not a penny less.

The MRP theory of wages continues to be taught by academic economists and treated as orthodoxy by most libertarian ideologues and free-market conservatives, as well as many center-left neoliberals in the United States. In a defense of welfare payments that compensate for low wages for workers, James Pethokoukis of the American Enterprise Institute invokes the theory: "Economics won't be ignored. If workers at a big profitable company only generate $10 an hour of revenue, then the company won't pay them $15 an hour."[4]

The MRP theory of wage determination may approximate reality in a few cases. In a fast-food restaurant, it might be possible to correlate sales with how many hamburgers particular workers make per hour. But how is it possible to specify the individual contributions to the annual global sales of a multinational corporation like Boeing of an executive secretary, a vice president for marketing, and a production engineer? It can't be done.

Nevertheless, the bipartisan American economic elite has taken the human capital theory to heart. And with good reason, from its perspective. The human capital story shifts any responsibility for low wages from employers or government policies. The theory can be invoked as proof that all wages are accurate and objective reflections of worker contribution to profits, based on worker skills. It is inevitable that some nursing aides and janitors will be paid poverty wages—so the story goes. To interfere with the automatic operations of the allegedly free labor market—for example, by unionizing nursing aides and janitors or raising the federal, state, or local minimum wages—would only backfire. Therefore, if nursing aides or janitors want to improve their wages, they should not even think about collective labor action or political campaigns. Instead, they should focus on upgrading their own personal skills, by gaining more vocational or college education, and switching to a better-paid profession. In particular, they should obtain skills in STEM (science, technology, engineering, and math) vocations.

In other words, they should learn to code.

The other story—the correct one—is the worker power theory of wage determination. If wages, along with other elements of jobs such as hours and benefits, do not correspond directly to an individual worker's measurable productivity, then how are wages set? They are set by bargaining.

We often assume that prices are set only by markets or, for some goods, by government regulation, but that is wrong. In the real world, prices can be, and often are, set by a third method: negotiation among two or more parties.

A bazaar provides an illustration. What is the price of a rug in a vendor's booth? The price of the rug is whatever the vendor and the buyer can agree on. Vendor and buyer may reach agreement only after a prolonged process of bargaining, during which the would-be buyer may threaten to walk away. The vendor may insist several times that this is a final offer before capitulating and offering a lower price to lure the departing buyer back. The point is that there is no objective price of that particular rug.

The role of bargaining in setting prices is familiar in many areas. Often a large group, negotiating as a unit, can get better prices than isolated individuals. A trade association planning a convention can get discounts for its members from a hotel. A large corporation can get discounts for health insurance for its employees that are not offered to small businesses or self-employed individuals. Labor unions seek to use collective bargaining to get higher wages for their members than any isolated individual worker could obtain.

Academic economists, along with the policy makers and pundits whom they teach, frequently claim that collective bargaining among organized labor and single or allied employers threatens economic efficiency, by raising the price of labor above its single, true market price. But in most markets of all kinds, *there is no single, true market price.*

Neoclassical economics is based on the idea of "general equilibrium": prices are magically and automatically set by simultaneous auctions among countless buyers and sellers throughout an entire economy. Among other things, equilibrium theory assumes zero or near-zero profits, with perfect competition driving down profits to match costs. In almost all markets for all goods and services in the real world, profits exceed costs considerably. If they did not, nobody would want to go into that line of business.

The most famous classical liberal economist, Adam Smith, recognized that prices, including wages, may be indeterminate within a broad range and must be "fixed by the higgling of the market." Smith observed that in negotiations over wages employers usually have much greater bargaining power than individual workers: "In the long-run, the workman may be as necessary to his master as his master is to him; but the necessity is not so immediate."[5]

A later classical liberal, J. S. Mill, agreed that wages are set by "what Adam Smith calls the 'higgling of the market.'"[6] This being the case, Mill asked, "What chance would any labourer have who struck singly for an advance of wages?" Mill concluded: "I do not hesitate to say that associations of labourers, of a nature similar to trade unions, far from being a hindrance to a free market for labour, are the necessary instrumentality of that free market; the indispensable means of enabling the sellers of labour to take due care of their own interest under a system of competition."[7] A few generations later, Alfred Marshall, a transitional figure between classical and neoclassical economics, agreed: "It is this unfairness of bad masters which makes unions necessary and gives them their chief force."[8]

The human capital theory of American wage polarization is not supported by international comparative studies. The human capital theory holds that the polarization of wages and jobs in the United States is the inevitable result of technological and economic forces. If this were true, the same worldwide forces should produce similar results in all advanced industrial economies. In reality, however, the growth of inequality in wages as well as wealth has been far more extreme in the United States than in western Europe or East Asia, suggesting that purely domestic American institutional factors must be important.

While it has occurred to some degree in all Western countries in the neoliberal era, the assault on worker bargaining power in the private sector has been taken to an extreme in the United States. Union membership remains higher in most European democracies.[9]

Other English-speaking countries tend to share America's pro-market and antigovernment traditions. Among Western democracies, anti-union neoliberalism in economic policy was strongest under Thatcher and Reagan and similar politicians in Anglophone nations. Even so, private sector union membership in 2021 was 13.8 percent in Canada and 12.8 percent in the UK, about twice as high as the roughly 6 percent private sector unionization rate in the United States.[10] In the nineteenth century the United States was unique among Western countries for the bloody violence of its labor conflicts. Today the United States is unique among developed nations when it comes to the thoroughness with which the economic overclass has decimated the bargaining power of the multiracial working-class majority.

A study of eighteen advanced economies, including that of the United States, by the International Monetary Fund between 1981 and 2010 concluded that 40 percent of the rise in the income share of the top 10 percent could be attributed to union decline.[11] In the United States, the decline of unions might have been responsible for 20 percent of the rise in earnings inequality among male workers in the 1980s.[12] One study estimated that one-fifth to one-third of the growth in wage inequality in the United States between 1973 and 2007 was the result of de-unionization.[13]

In 2008 and 2011, reports by the Organization for Economic

Cooperation and Development (OECD) claimed that pretax incomes in the United States and the European Union are similar; Europe is more equal only because of greater after-tax transfers through the welfare state. This argument reinforced the tendency of American neoliberal Democrats to ignore issues of worker power and focus their energy on increasing redistributive after-tax social spending to supplement low wages. It also strengthened the neoliberal consensus, by appearing to support the view that lower wages were caused everywhere by impersonal global economic or technological forces and that nothing could be done except to provide more government welfare for the poorly paid.

In 2020, however, three scholars—Thomas Blanchet, Lucas Chancel, and Amory Gethin—took another look at the data and declared that the OECD had been wrong. In fact, both pretax and post-tax inequality rose much more in the United States than in Europe between 1980 and 2017. Between two-thirds and 90 percent of the difference is caused by more equal European wages, according to the study.

> Contrary to a widespread view, we demonstrate that Europe's lower inequality levels cannot be explained by more equalizing tax-and-transfer systems. After accounting for indirect taxes and in-kind transfers, the US redistributes a greater share of national income to low-income groups than any European country. "Predistribution," not "redistribution," explains why Europe is less unequal than the United States.[14]

"If anything, taxes and transfers reduce inequality more in the US than in Europe," the authors conclude.

The main reason for the uniquely bad record of the United States in creating large numbers of low-wage jobs must be sought in institutional factors unique to the United States. And the most significant factors are those that shape the relative bargaining power of employers and workers, with the degree of unionization being the most important.

Nine years after claiming that wage inequality was due to "people . . . being treated closer to the way that they're supposed to be treated," Larry Summers abandoned the human capital theory in a 2020 study published with the Harvard economist Anna Stansbury. In "The Declining Worker Power Hypothesis: An Explanation for the Recent Evolution of the American Economy," they write, "By worker power, we mean workers' ability to increase their pay above the level that would prevail in the absence of such bargaining power. In this framework, worker power not only acts as countervailing power to firm monopsony power but also gives workers an ability to receive a share of the rents generated by companies operating in imperfectly competitive product markets."[15] In other words, workers in some fortunate sectors can share the market power of the firms that employ them, as we have seen already.

Summers and Stansbury rejected the theory that sectoral changes—from manufacturing to services, for example—could explain the decline in labor rents.[16] They also dismissed globalization and the increasing concentration of business as the main cause, as opposed to contributing factors. They concluded: "The evidence in this paper suggests that the American economy has become more ruthless, as declining unionization, increasingly demanding and empowered shareholders, decreasing real minimum wages, reduced worker protections, and the increases in outsourcing domestically and abroad have disempowered workers—with profound consequences for the labor market and the broader economy." The fact that even a neoliberal economist as influential as Larry Summers now endorses the worker bargaining power theory of wage inequality is an encouraging sign that the human capital theory can now be criticized even within the American establishment.[17]

Notwithstanding the attempts of the economic elite to distract us with misleading explanations for low wages in the United States, worker bargaining power remains the central issue. Certain institutions and policies increase worker power and diminish the bargaining power of employers—among them, a high degree of labor union membership, or at least coverage, by collective bargaining agreements; limits on the ability of firms to avoid paying high wages by moving jobs out of the country or importing immigrants willing to work for lower pay in worse conditions than native and naturalized workers; high federal and state minimum wages; and a system of unemployment insurance and other social insurance that allows individual workers to "hold out" longer while waiting for employers to give in and raise wages.

Other institutions and policies have the opposite effect. They diminish worker power and increase the bargaining power of employers—among them, de-unionization; government trade and investment treaties that make it easier to offshore jobs; government immigration policies that expand low-wage legal immigration or fail to enforce sanctions against hiring illegal immigrants; allowing inflation to lower the value of federal, state, and local minimum wages year after year; and a system of public assistance that compels its recipients to work at poverty-wage jobs, trapping them in a limbo in which they may never be able to earn enough to be free from public assistance.

Worker protections did not gradually disappear from the 1980s to the present as a result of allegedly irresistible forces of technology or globalization. The protections were deliberately eliminated, by U.S. employers and the government policy makers of both parties who acted as their agents. As we will see, evading and destroying American organized labor was one of the motives, if not the major motive, of the business lobbies that pressured the federal government to rewrite U.S. trade and immigration laws to facilitate both mass offshoring and mass immigration. How American employer lobbies and their allies in government have destroyed worker power in the United States in the last half century is the subject of the next four chapters.

CHAPTER TWO

The Bad End of the Bargain

How Organized Labor in the Private Sector Was Destroyed

I n 2005, Steve Jobs gave a commencement address at Stanford University. His advice to the graduates on how to find success is now famous:

> You've got to find what you love. And that is as true for your
> work as it is for your lovers. . . . As with all matters of your
> heart, you'll know it when you find it. And, like any great re-
> lationship, it just gets better and better as the years roll on. So
> keep looking until you find it. Don't settle.[1]

Inspirational words, to be sure. Unfortunately, what enabled Jobs to find what he loved and to build the empire that is Apple is less noble. Around the time that he gave this speech, Jobs was secretly acting as the ringleader to a massive conspiracy among employers in Silicon Valley to suppress the wages of professional tech workers. In addition, Jobs and his successors oversaw the off-shoring of Apple iPhone assembly to China and the sourcing of many of its supply chains in low-wage countries. Apple profited from the labor of H-1B indentured servants from other countries who had fewer rights and often lower wages than their American co-workers.[2] And today Apple, advised by America's largest anti-union law firm, Littler Mendelson, is notorious for the use of "captive audience meetings" and other tactics to intimidate workers at its stores in the United States in order to prevent them from joining unions.[3]

In his hostility to worker power, Jobs was typical of the leaders of the Silicon Valley tech industry. One of the inventors of the microchip, Robert Noyce, known as "the Mayor of Silicon Valley," declared that "remaining non-union is essential for survival for most of our companies. If we had the work rules that unionized companies have, we'd all go out of business."[4]

The claim that the information technology revolution was somehow incompatible with collective bargaining and robust worker rights was always a self-serving myth, spread by tech executives and investors and the politicians, journalists, and intellectuals whom they impressed, bribed, or deceived. Somehow in the 1960s the Defense Department created ARPANET, which became the internet, without using serf labor overseas. Portable phones with video attached to the internet would exist today in some form, even if Apple and others had not outsourced much of their production to China and other low-wage countries. Maybe the phones would cost slightly more, but the cost would be worth it to have a larger U.S. industrial base and fewer Americans in other sectors who can only survive with the help of government welfare programs.

Steve Jobs, Bill Gates, Google's founders, Larry Page and Sergey Brin, Mark Zuckerberg, and others have been brilliant and creative entrepreneurs, but they and others have modified and diffused technological innovations funded between the 1940s and the 1970s by the Defense Department and pioneered by Bell Labs, an agency of a regulated public utility, AT&T, and a few other big corporations like IBM and Xerox. Their fortunes, and the tax-free foundations many of these tech tycoons have created to impose their personal policy preferences on society, were the result of luck and timing, in winner-take-all races in which they happened to be only slightly ahead of the competition. The tragedy of our time is that the leading American industry, in terms of prestige if not of employment, should be one as hostile to worker rights and worker power as the tech industry of Silicon Valley.

In 2021, 68 percent of Americans approved of labor unions, a number higher than at any time since the 1960s. For the entire period between 1937 and 2021, the number of Americans who support unions has never dipped below half, except during the financial crisis of 2009 that began the Great Recession, when it fell to 48 percent. Meanwhile, membership in private sector labor unions in the United States declined from 35.7 percent in 1953 to 6.2 percent in 2019. American employers decimated private sector union membership over the past half century despite the pro-union attitudes of most Americans, including many Republicans.

At their zenith in 1954, following the promotion of unionization during the New Deal and World War II by the Roosevelt administration and Congress, labor unions represented more than a third of wage and salary workers in the United States, almost all of them in the private sector. By 1983, union membership had declined to 20.1 percent of wage and salary workers. In 2021, only 10.3 percent of American workers of all kinds belonged to unions and only 6.1 percent of private sector workers.[5]

In absolute numbers, union members in 2019 were divided almost evenly between the public sector (7.1 million) and the private sector (7.5 million). But the rate of unionization was much higher in the public sector (33.6 percent) than in the private sector (6.2 percent). The remaining unionized workers in the private sector are more likely to be found in utilities (23.4 percent) and transportation and warehousing (16.1 percent) than in food services (1.4 percent). More than half of U.S. union members live in only seven states that account for one-third of national wage and salary employment: California, New York, Illinois, Pennsylvania, New Jersey, Ohio, and Washington.[6]

It is a sign of how far organized labor has fallen that today American unions represent a smaller share of private sector workers

THE BAD END OF THE BARGAIN

than they did in 1935, before the enactment of the National Labor Relations Act during the New Deal.

This did not come about by accident. In low-wage/high-welfare America, union busting is a flourishing industry. American companies seeking to defeat unionization drives can hire management consultants that specialize in union avoidance, law firms, personnel psychologists, and strike management firms, the heirs to the Pinkerton agency, which American capitalists used to intimidate workers in the nineteenth and early twentieth centuries.[7] In 2019, the Economic Policy Institute estimated that U.S. firms spend around $340 million a year in fees to union avoidance experts, used by 75 percent of all companies confronted by union elections involving fifty or more workers.[8]

The law firm of Littler Mendelson has provided Apple and Starbucks with tips on fighting pro-union employee efforts.[9] In addition to advising American corporations, Littler provides its services to foreign multinationals with sites and employees in the United States. Littler helped Nissan defeat unionization efforts at its automobile plants in Smyrna, Tennessee, and Canton, Mississippi, between 2014 and 2017.[10]

In its campaign against unionization, Amazon paid several consulting firms. One of them, Lev Labor, charged a weekly rate of $20,000 for its consultants, who, according to a scope-of-work letter, would try to discourage workers from unionizing by means of "meetings," "walk-throughs," and "focus groups."[11] Amazon has also hired the Labor Relations Institute, a union avoidance consulting firm that has helped the Amazon-owned Whole Foods thwart unionization.[12]

In response to employee activism that began in 2018, Google secretly began Project Vivian, which one manager in court-obtained documents described as an effort to "convince them that unions suck." As part of this effort, in 2019 Google hired IRI Consultants, a notorious union-busting firm.[13] While working in 2019 to prevent unionization at two hospitals in Seattle owned by Conifer Health Solutions, IRI Consultants secretly compiled information about eighty-three hospital employees to gauge their susceptibility to pro-union appeals, describing one as "from Samoa," "lazy," and "money oriented," and another as "a single mother" who could not "afford [union] dues" because her "rent [had] increased."[14]

One scholar observes, "The USA is alone among rich democracies in allowing the development of an enormous industry of law firms dedicated to defeating union organising campaigns and keeping their clients—including many large multinational corporations—union free." The four largest U.S. law firms that specialize in union avoidance strategies, with lawyers spread throughout the country and the world to be near their clients, are Ogletree Deakins, Littler Mendelson, Jackson Lewis, and Fisher Phillips.[15] Several of these have taken part in the tech industry's battles against unionization.

One of Ogletree's clients, a cloud-based software company named Lanetix, forced its employees to attend so-called "captive meetings" at which they were told by the CEO and senior staff that workers who took part in union activity would be fired, while the jobs of others might be transferred to eastern Europe. After the National Labor Relations Board ruled that Lanetix had violated labor law, the firm admitted to breaking the law and paid fifteen coders a total of $775,000.[16]

Since the civil rights revolution, many American corporations have ostentatiously embraced symbolic race-and-gender identity politics in the form of affirmative action and multiculturalism, now called "diversity, equity, and inclusion" (DEI), even as they oppose unionization, a higher minimum wage, and other pro-worker legislation.

Critics on the left and right have long viewed this embrace of identity politics by corporations and banks as an effort by U.S. firms to divert attention from their antilabor practices, which hurt workers of all races, both sexes, and all sexual orientations. Now, according to the journalist Lee Fang, writing in *The Intercept*, companies and their union avoidance consultants have tried to co-opt the language of DEI in anti-union campaigns. Fang writes, "When workers at vegan food company No Evil Foods, which makes imitation meat products sold at Whole Foods and other upscale groceries, held captive audience anti-union seminars, the company warned workers about the 'old white guys' in union leadership and compared union dues to taxpayers funding President Donald Trump's golf junkets."

Some union-busting firms have even redefined themselves as diversity consultants. According to Fang, "One of the most insidious tactics have [*sic*] been the use of supposed employee resource groups, also known as affinity groups or ERGs [employee re-source groups], to undermine labor activism. Many companies offer specific ERGs for Asian, Black, Latino, or LGBTQ+ indi-viduals, among other identity-based suborganizations as part of a larger diversity and inclusion program." The union-busting consultant IRI, hired by Google among others, observes that "di-versity and inclusion (D&I) initiatives" can help to "union-proof your business." Fang notes that Danielle Brown, Google's chief diversity officer and leader of its ERG programs, made the deci-sion on behalf of Google to hire the anti-union services of IRI Consultants.[17]

In 1995, the British academics Richard Barbrook and Andy Cam-eron described what they called "the Californian ideology" of Silicon Valley:

> This new faith has emerged from a bizarre fusion of the cul-tural bohemianism of San Francisco with the hi-tech in-dustries of Silicon Valley. Promoted in magazines, books, TV programmes, websites, newsgroups and Net conferences, the Californian Ideology promiscuously combines the free-wheeling spirit of the hippies and the entrepreneurial zeal of the yuppies. This amalgamation of opposites has been achieved through a profound faith in the emancipatory potential of the new information technologies. In the digital utopia, every-

body will be both hip and rich. Not surprisingly, this optimistic vision of the future has been enthusiastically embraced by computer nerds, slacker students, innovative capitalists, social activists, trendy academics, futurist bureaucrats and opportunistic politicians across the USA.[18]

For the last generation, the anti-union tech industry and the equally anti-union Wall Street finance industry have showered donations on sycophants in the media, universities, and think tanks, promoting carefully crafted PR images of the tech entrepreneur or tech CEO as an iconoclastic, visionary, bohemian genius and of the investment bank or hedge fund executive as a chin-stroking, public-spirited "thought leader," to divert public attention from the war on worker power in these industries, whose practices set an example for many other businesses. Unfortunately, the digital utopia did not work out, and most people are neither hip nor rich. More and more Americans are coming to realize that amoral, venal robber barons can be found in jeans and T-shirts as well as in three-piece suits and top hats.

The successful campaign of the tech sector and other American industries to crush private sector unions is only part of the fifty-year war on American worker power from the 1980s onward. As we will see in the next three chapters, by methods like outsourcing, contractual clauses, offshoring, and importing cheap labor from abroad, the American business establishment has smashed the bargaining power of American workers, with harmful consequences for all of American society.

CHAPTER THREE

Boss Rule

How Employment Practices
Are Rigged Against Workers

Today around 94 percent of American workers in the private sector are not represented by labor unions. Without union representation, individual employees are all but powerless in negotiations with small and medium firms, much less national and global bureaucratic leviathans. You might think that American employers would be content with the weakness the near annihilation of organized labor in the private sector has produced, but you would be wrong. The decimation of private sector unions has not prevented many American companies from trying to weaken the bargaining power of their already weak workers further, by means of salary bands, no-poach agreements, non-compete clauses, forced arbitration, and the outsourcing of jobs to contractors, as we will see in this chapter.

SALARY BANDS

Let's begin with a technique used by many American businesses to limit the ability of workers to force employers to bid for their services. Salary bands in large, bureaucratic corporations and non-profits are set by informal collusion among different firms to fix common wage levels for workers in the whole industry or sector—in other words, by price-fixing at the expense of the bargaining power of their employees among the members of an employers' cartel.

To be sure, it's not called price-fixing, because price-fixing is illegal. Under U.S. antitrust law, it is against the law for employers to band together and agree on the same employee compensation policies, in order to allow the firms to present a united front to job seekers who might hope for a bidding war among employers competing to hire them.

In 2016, the Justice Department issued its "Antitrust Guidance for Human Resource Professionals," reminding corporate HR staffs that they cannot get together to set common prices for labor and thus undercut the bargaining power of workers:

An individual likely is breaking the antitrust laws if he or she:

- agrees with individual(s) at another company about employee salary or other terms of compensation, either at a specific level or within a range (so-called wage-fixing agreements), or

- agrees with individual(s) at another company to refuse to solicit or hire that other company's employees (so-called "no poaching" agreements).[1]

The American business community has come up with ingenious ways to set salaries on the basis of salary bands shared by multiple firms, without crossing the line into blatantly illegal wage fixing. Many U.S. firms hire third parties such as consultants to tell them what other companies are doing, rather than asking other companies directly. In other cases, HR officers set salary bands on the basis of Bureau of Labor Statistics data about average salaries in particular occupations. (I doubt that the founders of BLS intended for its statistics to be used to create anti-worker hiring cartels.)

Astron Solutions, a consulting firm that specializes in HR issues, provides a list of ways that firms can dance along the cliff edge of antitrust law violations without falling over:

> It can be difficult for Human Resources to explain and adhere to these anti-trust implications when a manager fears losing talented staff to a competitor. Here are some viable, proactive steps you can take now to obtain data and stay in compliance with the law:
>
> 1. Work with local SHRM, WorldatWork, or other Human Resource organization chapters to offer confidential annual and quarterly "hot job" salary surveys, with the data compiled by a disassociated third party.

2. Work with the local Chamber of Commerce or Industrial Association to develop a similar survey process.

3. Invite competitors to meet with a disassociated third party to create a confidential survey group.

4. Incorporate "new salary" questions into your exit analysis process to track where employees are going and for what salary level.

5. Survey potential employees who reject offers to determine if salary played a part in their decision.[2]

NO-POACH AGREEMENTS

These are secret agreements among firms to avoid "poaching" or hiring one another's employees. Illegal under federal antitrust laws, no-poaching agreements keep wages down throughout an entire occupation or industry, by preventing workers from forcing different employers to bid for their services with higher wages or benefits.

Leading firms in Silicon Valley and Hollywood, overwhelmingly Democratic and viewed as progressive in their politics, engaged in the biggest no-poach criminal conspiracy in history in the early twenty-first century. In 2017, Walt Disney, Pixar, and Lucasfilm Ltd. settled a lawsuit filed against them by animators by agreeing to pay $100 million; as part of the same lawsuit, Dream-Works had already paid $50 million, while Sony Pictures and other defendants paid a total of $19 million. In a related settlement in 2015, Google, Apple, Adobe, Intel, and other tech firms agreed to pay $415 million to settle a case involving their secret deal not to hire software engineers from one another.[3] In the latter case, the judge wrote, "There is substantial and compelling evidence that Steve Jobs . . . was a, if not the, central figure in the alleged conspiracy."[4]

On February 13, 2006, Jobs, then CEO of Apple, complained to Eric Schmidt, CEO of Google, that Google was recruiting workers from Apple's iPod Group: "If that is true, can you put a stop to it?" Schmidt replied, "I'm sorry to hear this; we have a policy of no recruiting of Apple employees. I will investigate immediately!"

Contacted by Schmidt, Google's director of staffing, Arnnon Geshuri, told him that the Google staffer "who contacted this Apple employee should not have and will be terminated within the hour." Three days later Google's senior vice president for business operations, Shona Brown, sent a note to Geshuri: "Please make a public example of this termination with the group."[5]

In 2017, the journalist Rachel Abrams shocked readers of *The New York Times* by revealing that the thirty-two largest fast-food chains in the United States, including McDonald's, Pizza Hut, Burger King, and Domino's, had their own no-poach agreements that prevented their franchises from hiring workers who had worked for other chains. The stipulations were hidden in agreements between the national companies and their franchisers.[6]

Who says that fast food is a backward industry, compared

with Silicon Valley tech? Even if they do not own superyachts and private jets, fast-food executives, it turns out, can use advanced tools of industry-wide wage suppression just as effectively as the CEOs of Apple and Google.

Modern machinery would have surprised the eighteenth-century economist Adam Smith, but not the machinations of modern employers:

> We rarely hear, it has been said, of the combinations of masters, though frequently of those of workers. But whoever imagines, upon this account, that masters rarely combine, is as ignorant of the world as of the subject. Masters are always and everywhere in a sort of tacit, but constant and uniform, combination, not to raise the wages of labour above their actual rate.[7]

NON-COMPETE CLAUSES

Non-compete clauses in an employment contract force the worker to agree not to go to work for rivals of the employer after quitting or being fired, for a certain period of time or forever. The original purpose of non-compete clauses was to protect the investments of professional firms in intellectual property and to prevent former employees from taking their clients with them.

In recent years, however, non-compete clauses have spread into contracts in many occupations. In 2021, 18 percent of American workers were bound by non-compete clauses and 38 percent had been forced to consent to one by an employer in the past.[8] Even fast-food workers have been forced to sign non-compete agreements, in a sign, perhaps, of the continuing diffusion of advanced worker-suppression techniques from Silicon Valley to the rest of the American economy.[9]

FORCED ARBITRATION

Forced arbitration is yet another practice that is only possible because of the lack of labor union representation or adequate labor laws. When being hired, workers must sign a clause promising not to sue the employer in the courts but only to use arbitration procedures, which tend to favor companies. As Susan Antilla notes in *Capital & Main*, more than sixty million Americans in the nonunion private sector workforce have been compelled to agree to these contractual clauses:

> That's a boon to companies looking to reduce damaging financial exposure: Based on research that estimates 98% of private sector, nonunion employees subject to arbitration will abandon their claims, a report by the National Employment Law Project calculated that, in 2019, more than 4.5 million workers who are subject to mandatory arbitration and making less than $13 an hour would fail to bring wage theft claims worth $9.27 billion.[10]

CONTRACT, OR "GIG," WORK

The 1947 Taft-Hartley Act, passed by an antilabor coalition in Congress, added exclusions of independent contractors and supervisors to the 1935 Wagner Act's exclusion of agricultural and domestic workers. Under the Taft-Hartley exclusions, employers can replace in-firm workers with independent contractors, restructuring their pay as "miscellaneous income" rather than taxable wages. Such maneuvering allows employers to escape many legal and financial obligations—Social Security and other payroll taxes, workers' compensation liability, minimum wage and overtime requirements, and others. Employers can also deny contractors the health insurance, pensions, and other benefits that are available to employees.

Many firms have used domestic outsourcing to replace well-paid full-time employees with benefits with poorly paid contractors or temporary workers. At the same time, American employers have shifted the cost and risk of benefits to workers—for example, by replacing defined-benefit pensions with defined-contribution pensions like 401(k)s—or to the American taxpayer, by avoiding or shedding the provision of employer-based health insurance. Firms like Uber and Lyft and DoorDash base their business models on outsourcing.

The result is what the economist David Weil calls "the fissured workplace," in which firms outsource more and more of their functions to contractors, in order to lower their wage and benefit costs and the cost of compliance with federal labor regulations.[11]

Suppose that a company fires its janitors to save money on their wages and benefits. Some of the janitors are then hired by a janitorial service company, one of several that compete for the business of the janitors' former company. The janitorial firm that pays its workers the least while providing no benefits will get the contract. In this way, outsourcing multiplies low-wage jobs while ensuring that full-time, well-paid managers and professionals, along with shareholders, enjoy a greater share of the gains of the corporation's growth. The situation will be even worse if the janitorial firm decides that it, too, wants to outsource its jobs to avoid labor laws and wages and hours laws and defines the janitor as a self-employed contractor, not an employee.

And if the former corporate janitors are unable to live on their earnings as involuntary self-employed contractors? They will be rescued from complete destitution by the welfare state, paid for by federal, state, and local taxpayers. At the risk of harping on the theme of this book (but what are harps for?), allow me to repeat: *the business model of twenty-first-century American neoliberal capitalism is privatizing the benefits and socializing the costs of cheap labor.*

Where did the money that companies saved by lowering labor costs go? Some of it appears to have been used to increase the number and salaries of corporate managers. From the mid-1980s until the early years of the twenty-first century, the share of total business income that went to managers rose from 16 to 23 percent; the proportional number of managers in the U.S. private sector increased; and hourly earnings for managers shot up by 34 percent over two decades, even as most wages stagnated.[12] Managerial earnings grew the most in goods-producing industries, suggesting that shares of the profits that had gone to well-paid, unionized production workers were redirected to managers. In his book *Fat and Mean: The Corporate Squeeze of Working Americans and the Myth of Managerial "Downsizing"* (1996), David Gordon conjectured that companies need more managers to supervise the low-wage, low-skilled workers who replaced better-paid and skilled unionized workers.[13] Replacing unionized employees with low-paid, disposable contract workers results in a race-to-the-bottom business model that benefits only affluent investors, managers, and professionals, along with consumers who in many cases are much better off than the financially struggling workers who serve them.

The examples of outsourcing to cut labor costs that I have discussed here are all domestic. But in their quest to pay workers the lowest possible wages, many corporations have engaged in "offshore outsourcing" or "offshoring"—the transfer of the production of goods or services to low-wage, non-union workers in other countries, who work either for third-party contractors or for affiliates of the corporation. The widespread use of offshoring by American employers to weaken or destroy American unions and replace American workers with foreign workers is the subject of the next chapter.

CHAPTER FOUR

Global Labor Arbitrage I

How Employers Use Offshoring to Crush Worker Power

In *Capital Moves: RCA's Seventy-Year Quest for Cheap Labor* (1999), Jefferson Cowie documents the journey of a once-great American corporation in search of low-wage, non-union workers. The major electronics manufacturer RCA repeatedly chose factory sites in low-wage areas, only to abandon them for new ones once the workers tried to organize. In this way RCA shifted some of its production from Camden, New Jersey, to Bloomington, Indiana, and then Memphis, Tennessee, before finding an even cheaper workforce in Ciudad Juárez, Mexico.[1] At the same time, RCA, which had led in the development of global television technology and manufacturing, was licensing its technology to East Asian firms. Today the United States no longer makes televisions and RCA no longer exists.

The economist Alan Blinder is a former member of President Bill Clinton's Council of Economic Advisers and a former vice-chairman of the Board of Governors of the Federal Reserve System who went on to make a personal fortune in the finance industry following his service as a government financial regulator. In 2009 Blinder declared,

> The TV manufacturing industry really started here, and at one point employed many workers. But as TV sets became "just a commodity," their production moved offshore to locations with much lower wages. And nowadays the number of television sets manufactured in the U.S. is zero. A failure? No, a success.[2]

The offshoring of manufacturing labor that RCA and hundreds of other American companies have undertaken was prophetically foretold in 1934 by an influential historian, Charles A. Beard. In a polemic titled *The Open Door at Home: A Trial Philosophy of National Interest*, Beard predicted that the abolition of tariffs and other protectionist measures by the nations of the world and the creation of a global free market, a goal of idealistic American and European liberal internationalists, would not result in great numbers of foreign consumers purchasing products made by well-paid American workers, as promised. Instead, corporations with headquarters in the United States and elsewhere would relocate production to other nations to take advantage of cheap labor: "Under world free trade there would be a movement of manufacturing industries from the regions in which wages are high, social legislation is strict, and trade unions are powerful to the backward regions where wages are low, social legislation negligible if not absent, and labor unorganized."[3]

This is exactly what has happened, in the last half century, between the 1980s and the present. It did not happen in the three decades that immediately followed World War II, because of the protectionism of postcolonial countries, Western embargos on the communist bloc, and the devastation of America's major industrial rivals by the war. Unable to offshore production to a significant degree, American manufacturers often engaged in regional geographic arbitrage within the United States to thwart unionization. One company after another transferred production from union-friendly states in the Northeast and Midwest to states in the South and West whose governments had "right-to-work" laws that were hostile to organized labor. These states used the poverty of their workers along with low taxes as bait to lure corporate investment.

After the end of the cold war, Charles Beard's prophecy finally came true. Communism was abandoned formally in the former Soviet Union and jettisoned in practice by nominally Marxist-Leninist China. Ex-communist countries and former members of the cold war–era nonaligned bloc invited U.S., European, and Japanese corporations to hire their low-wage workers.

Under Republican and Democratic presidents alike, the United States pushed through a series of so-called free trade agreements—the North American Free Trade Agreement (NAFTA) in 1994, the World Trade Organization (WTO) in 1995, and permanent normal trade relations (PNTR) with China, which opened up China's low-wage labor pool to U.S. companies. These lengthy, detailed "free trade agreements" had little to do with free trade. They were regulatory harmonization agreements that made it easier for Western multinationals to transfer production to poor and non-unionized workers in other countries, some of them repressive dictatorships like China and Vietnam.

In 2007, President Alan García of Peru, during a speech to the U.S. Chamber of Commerce, made an offer to American businesses of a kind made by many other leaders of low-wage nations: "Come and open your factories in my country so we can sell your own products back to the U.S."[4]

G lobal arbitrage" refers to the ability of firms or investors to profit by exploiting differences between jurisdictions in regulations, taxes, or wages. Global labor arbitrage comes in two forms: offshoring (moving production to foreign workers in order to pay lower wages) and leveraging immigration (bringing foreign workers into the country who are willing to work for less than native or naturalized workers). In the past half century, both offshoring and immigration have been weaponized and used against American workers on a massive scale by American firms in various industries that have adopted one or both of these labor arbitrage strategies to crush worker bargaining power and minimize labor costs.

During the heyday of globalization in the 1990s and first decade of the twenty-first century, those who addressed elite business audiences were sometimes quite candid in stating that the goal of offshoring was to boost corporate profits by replacing high-wage American workers with low-wage foreign workers.

Walter Wriston, the chair and CEO of Citicorp and author of a neoliberal manifesto titled *The Twilight of Sovereignty* (1992), was also honest: "When steel mills can move to more hospitable climates, they no longer present a stationary target for government or union control."[5] Just as honest was Jack Welch, the CEO of General Electric, who declared in 1998, "Ideally, you'd have every plant you own on a barge."[6]

But such brutal candor was rare. Trying to minimize the role of cheap labor in offshoring and imports in the collapse of U.S. manufacturing employment in the early twenty-first century, many economists, echoed by neoliberal pundits in the media, claimed that the loss of manufacturing jobs was almost entirely the result of automation. This was an implausible assertion, inasmuch as Detroit and many other U.S. manufacturing centers by the 2010s were decaying slums, not thriving communities with newly upgraded robotic factories and well-paid employees, as the automation explanation for U.S. deindustrialization would suggest.

Scholarship soon discredited the "automation did it" alibi for cheap-labor globalization. In a 2016 study, David H. Autor, David

Dorn, and Gordon H. Hanson demonstrated that "the China shock" was indeed responsible for much of the rapid decline in U.S. manufacturing jobs: "At the national level, employment has fallen in U.S. industries more exposed to import competition, as expected, but offsetting employment gains in other industries have yet to materialize."[7] Then, in 2018, Susan N. Houseman showed that those who attributed the decline of American manufacturing jobs primarily to productivity growth rather than trade had mistakenly treated U.S. imports of computers and computer components as evidence of U.S. manufacturing productivity growth.[8]

If automation of American factories explained the dramatic drop in U.S. manufacturing employment in the early twenty-first century, then there should be more American robots than there are. Instead, South Korea is number one when it comes to "robot density," followed by Singapore, Japan, Germany, Sweden, Hong Kong, the United States, Taiwan, mainland China and Denmark (tied for ninth), and Italy. While South Korea has 932 industrial robots per 10,000 employees, the United States has only 255.[9] If automation leads to a declining share of the workforce in manufacturing and related industrial fields, then a much smaller percentage of South Korea's workforce should work in industry than in the United States. Instead, in 2019, 24.58 percent of South Korea's workforce was in manufacturing and 70.28 percent in services, compared with 19.91 percent in industry and 78.74 percent in services in the United States, using the same definition of industry.[10] Like South Korea, the countries that have the highest robot density tend to be those that have sought to preserve at least some domestic manufacturing industries by modernizing and up-grading factories instead of offshoring them.

Not content to invoke mystical and irresistible forces like technology in arguing that globalization was inevitable, some neoliberals claimed that corporate offshoring was humanitarian in its effects if not its motives. In the neoliberal magazine *Slate* in 1997, Paul Krugman published an essay titled "In Praise of Cheap Labor: Bad Jobs at Bad Wages Are Better Than No Jobs at All." Krugman declared, "While fat-cat capitalists might benefit from globalization, the biggest beneficiaries are, yes, Third World workers." According to Krugman, poor countries could modernize as prosperity trickled down from low-wage sweatshop workers doing contract work for multinational corporations to the rest of a backward agrarian economy:

> More importantly, however, the growth of manufacturing—and of the penumbra of other jobs that the new export sector creates—has a ripple effect throughout the economy. The pressure on the land becomes less intense, so rural wages rise; the pool of unemployed urban dwellers always anxious for work shrinks, so factories start to compete with each other for workers, and urban wages also begin to rise. Where the process has gone on long enough—say, in South Korea or Taiwan—average wages start to approach what an American teen-ager

can earn at McDonald's. And eventually people are no longer
eager to live on garbage dumps.[11]

Krugman's implication that the economic development of
South Korea and Taiwan was a gradual, market-driven by-product
of cheap-labor offshoring by foreign multinationals is at odds with
reality. The East Asian development model that led to the success
of Japan, South Korea, and Taiwan, a variant of the successful
state-sponsored industrialization strategies of the U.K., the United
States, and Germany, was based on government-imposed land reform that created a mass market of family farmers for industrial
goods, combined with systematic government promotion of infant industries by means of tariffs, nontariff barriers, and targeted
tariffs. These policies in turn were combined with a focus on export promotion, once protected and subsidized national industries
were mature enough to compete in world markets—all under the
direction of a strong and competent national government.[12]

Successful East Asian states have sometimes used export-
processing zones (EPZs) in which national workers have done contract work for multinational corporations, but only as temporary
measures to transfer technology and skills to their own workers
and business leaders, while building up their own protected and
subsidized national industries.[13] For example, Taiwan used EPZs
as part of an effective state-led strategy of import substitution development to promote its infant industries at the expense of foreign importers.[14] The Taiwanese government raised the amount
of Taiwanese-made inputs into EPZ manufacturing from 2.1 per-

cent in 1967 to a third by 1980. South Korea's Machinery Purchase Fund financed the purchase of South Korean industrial machinery for use in the EPZs instead of imported foreign equipment.[15]

In the two countries cited by Krugman in his 1997 *Slate* essay, Taiwan and South Korea, workers and managers were trained by multinationals in the EPZs and then transferred to protected or subsidized national industrial sectors, bringing the skills they had learned to national corporations that would compete with Japanese and Western companies. In other words, foreign multinationals based in the United States and Europe, driven by short-term greed, were manipulated by strong East Asian developmental states to create national companies that would seek to drive Western multinationals out of their domestic markets and then battle them in global markets. Thanks to their cheap-labor business strategies, American multinationals have sometimes helped to create their own foreign replacements and rivals. None of this bears any resemblance to Krugman's neoliberal fantasy of prosperity trickling down from poor workers in sweatshops to even poorer workers on garbage dumps.

When all other arguments fail, defenders of corporate offshoring in pursuit of low labor costs and high profits for managers and shareholders invoke the real or alleged benefits to American consumers. In a report titled "Offshoring: Is It a Win-Win Game?" the McKinsey Global Institute (MGI) conceded that some American workers would suffer from losing their jobs to low-wage workers in other countries. MGI proposed helping these displaced workers by means of a generous compensatory insurance system that—surprise!—never materialized.

As for the benefits of offshoring, according to MGI they would go to investors and consumers, not workers: "Initially, the savings [from lower wages for foreign workers] will flow to investors, or they will be invested in innovations or new business ventures. Eventually, as offshoring becomes more prevalent, competition will yield the savings to consumers." With pseudoscientific precision, MGI even calculated the precise dollar amount that the United States benefits from offshoring: "Far from being bad for the United States, offshoring creates net additional value for the U.S. economy that did not exist before, a full 12–14 cents on every dollar offshored."[16]

In 2014, Stephen Roach, the former chairman of Morgan Stanley Asia, similarly argued that the offshoring of industry to China was a win for both American companies and American consumers: "The benefits of such 'labor-cost arbitrage' are considerable. According to the U.S. Bureau of Labor Statistics, compensation in Chinese manufacturing averaged just $1.36 per hour in 2008— or only about 4 percent of the hourly rate of $34 paid by manufacturing companies in the United States." And the cost savings to American consumers? "The U.S. Commerce Department has calculated that import prices of non-auto consumer goods rose just 5 percent from 2000 to 2011—less than half the cumulative

11.4 percent increase of prices for all consumer goods over the same period." Roach concludes: "The cruel calculus of globalization suggests that the potential number of beneficiaries—namely, more than 310 million American consumers—vastly exceeds the 12 million manufacturing workers who may feel the pressures of outsourcing head-on" along with many other workers "who provide goods and services to the displaced workers" and suffer as well.[17]

Offshoring plus a flood of imports turned formerly flourishing industrial regions in the American Midwest and Northeast and elsewhere into abandoned, decaying slums, shifted millions of American workers from the productive traded sector into low-productivity, non-traded service jobs, and ceded a growing number of global markets to Chinese exporters. But look on the bright side: American consumers paid around *6 percent less* for imports from China than they might have paid for American-made products. What a bargain!

In discussing the benefits versus the costs of offshoring and low-wage immigration, neoliberal globalist authors like the MGI researchers and Roach engage in statistical trickery. They treat the benefits of lower prices to *particular* American consumers as gains for *all* American consumers. If some Americans buy foreign-made sneakers that are cheaper because they are made by unfree, repressed labor in communist Vietnam, this is accounted as a net benefit for every American.

But how is this possible? If you save money by buying imported serf-made sneakers, and I don't wear sneakers, in what sense have I or "Americans" in general benefited? You are the one with the cheap sneakers, not me or your fellow Americans.

From the standpoint of neoliberal globalists, this misleading argument is a great public relations gimmick. Using this trick, neoliberal propagandists can argue that only a few American workers are hurt by globalization but all American consumers benefit. The math of what Stephen Roach calls the "cruel calculus of globalization" would produce different results if the economic harm done to specific American workers from offshoring or imports was assigned to all American workers, while the economic benefit was limited to specific American consumers of specific imports.

Offshoring of production is only one form of global labor arbitrage used by corporations to evade organized labor and to lower labor costs. Another is the use of immigration to bring in foreign workers to perform jobs for low wages in the United States, instead of exporting jobs to low-wage workers abroad. How American employers have weaponized U.S. immigration policy, exploiting immigrants while harming native and foreign-born American citizen-workers, is the subject of the next chapter.

CHAPTER FIVE

Global Labor Arbitrage II

How Employers Exploit Immigrants to Weaken Worker Power

The subject of this chapter is the weaponization of immigration policies by American employers in their never-ending campaign to weaken American worker power. Most American workers have been affected more by de-unionization and anti-worker labor laws than by offshoring or immigration. But while the effects of pro-employer immigration policies should not be exaggerated, it is intellectually dishonest to ignore the harm done by immigration arbitrage strategies to substantial numbers of American workers, from farmworkers and janitors to professionals in the tech sector.

In treating immigration as a matter of labor economics, rather than as a matter of antiracist social justice, I am violating perhaps the greatest taboo of the bipartisan neoliberal regime that has ruled the United States since Reagan and Clinton. The overclass left, the neoliberal center, and the libertarian right all insist that immigration has only beneficial effects on American workers and the American economy; to question this establishment dogma is heresy.

This bipartisan consensus in favor of mass immigration dates back only to around 2000. For most of American history, labor union members tended to favor restrictive immigration policies, to create a seller's market in labor, while employers tended to favor higher levels of immigration, to create a buyer's market in labor. The older center-left position was reflected in the Carter administration's commission on immigration, chaired by the Reverend Theodore Hesburgh, and in the Clinton administration's commission, chaired by the African American politician Barbara Jordan. Both of these Democratic commissions called for cracking down on illegal immigration and reducing high levels of unskilled legal immigration, in order to protect low-wage American workers from immigrant competition. Their recommendations were opposed at the time by cheap-labor business interests and libertarian ideologues in the Republican Party.

The movement of the Democratic Party away from immigration skepticism and trade skepticism in the last generation has had several causes. One is the replacement of private sector union members as the social base of the Democratic Party by college-educated professionals and managers, who do not face immigrant competition or the threat of offshoring, and who often benefit from cheap imports made in foreign sweatshops and an abundant local supply of low-wage household servants and service workers. Another cause is the growing domination of the labor movement by public sector unions, whose members, like schoolteachers and government officials, have jobs that cannot be offshored or given to unskilled immigrant workers. Yet a third factor has been the hope that mass immigration would ensure a permanent Democratic majority, on the theory that Hispanic, Asian, and other non-European immigrants who became citizens and their descendants would form a bloc of "voters of color" allied permanently with white progressives. These three factors explain why the Democratic left now echoes the propaganda about immigration that continues to be associated with cheap-labor business lobbies and the libertarian right, including the charge that any criticism of high levels of immigration of any kind must be motivated by racism.

The fact remains that a wary attitude toward immigration on the part of organized labor in the past was often justified. As we have seen, the major form of worker power takes the form of collective bargaining by organized labor. The economist Vernon M. Briggs Jr. writes, "With only two exceptions [1897–1905 and 1922–1929], membership in American unions has over time moved inversely with trends in the size of immigration inflows."[1]

In 2022, the Cato Institute, an anti-union, libertarian think tank in Washington, D.C., published a study titled "Immigrants Reduce Unionization in the United States." Confirming the findings of Briggs, the study argued that immigration has played a major role in de-unionization in America: "We find that immigration reduced union density by 5.7 percentage points between 1980 and 2020, *which accounts for 29.7 percent of the overall decline in union density during that period* [emphasis added]." The study argues that mass immigration's effect on unionization is indirect. By increasing the ethnic diversity of the workforce, immigration increases mutual suspicion among groups and makes interracial and interethnic class solidarity more difficult.[2]

This would come as no surprise to Whole Foods, a company owned by Amazon that is notorious for its hostility to organized labor. Whole Foods has used computer-generated "heat maps" to identify locations where workers were most likely to try to unionize. The company discovered that stores with high levels of racial and ethnic diversity were less likely to support unionization efforts than those whose employees were more homogeneous in background.[3]

Nor would the finding that immigration makes unionization more difficult surprise the leaders of organized labor or employers in earlier generations. In 1875, the manager of a Pittsburgh factory explained, "My experience has shown that Germans and Irish, Swedes, and what I denominate Buckwheats (young American country boys), judiciously mixed, make the most effective and tractable force you can find."[4] In 1911, the U.S. Immigration Commission observed that "in many cases the conscious policy of the employers [is] mixing the races [white ethnic groups] in certain departments and divisions . . . preventing concert of action on the part of employees."[5]

It is racist and xenophobic to ask why businesses and employer lobbies almost without exception favor higher levels of immigration of all kinds, including legal immigrants and temporary guest workers, and oppose employer sanctions and other deterrents to hiring illegal immigrants—at least that is what America's corporate elite and corporate media and the co-opted progressive movement want us to believe.

Although white racism and Anglo-American Protestant ethnic and religious bigotry shaped U.S. immigration policies from the founding to the mid-twentieth century, African Americans and Hispanic Americans have often opposed high levels of immigration because of the harmful effects on low-income workers in their communities. In the nineteenth and twentieth centuries, for example, European immigrants competed with African Americans in many occupations, often to the detriment of the latter.

A. Philip Randolph, the founder of the Brotherhood of Sleeping Car Porters and the leading figure behind the integration of defense production in World War II and the March on Washington for Jobs and Freedom in 1963, was perhaps the greatest American civil rights activist of the twentieth century, along with Martin Luther King Jr. In 1924, Randolph called for race-neutral immigration reductions that would benefit workers of all races in the United States:

Instead of reducing immigration to 2 percent of the 1890 quota, we favor reducing it to nothing.... We favor shutting out the Germans from Germany, the Italians from Italy ... the Hindus from India, the Chinese from China, and even the Negroes from the West Indies. This country is suffering from immigrant indigestion.... It is time to call a halt on this grand rush for American gold, which over-floods the labor market, resulting in lowering the standard of living, race-riots, and general social degradation. The excessive immigration is against the interests of the masses of all races and nationalities in the country—both foreign and native.[6]

Among Hispanic Americans polled in 2018 by Pew, the largest number (48 percent) thought that the number of legal immigrants coming to the United States was the right amount; only 14 percent wanted the number of immigrants increased, compared with 25 percent of Hispanic respondents who felt that the United States admitted too many immigrants.[7] According to a Harvard CAPS/Harris poll in 2018, 53 percent of Latinos favored immediately deporting anyone who crossed the border illegally, while 70 percent supported more restrictive immigration laws.[8] Opposition to illegal immigration explains part of the shift of many Hispanic voters toward the Republican Party under Trump and Biden.

For generations, many Mexican Americans along the southwestern border have opposed the use of Mexican migrant workers by American agribusiness to keep wages in their regions low and worker bargaining power weak. The League of United Latin

American Citizens and the American GI Forum, the most influential Mexican American organizations after World War II, lobbied Congress to crack down on farmers and ranchers who used illegal immigrant labor. In 1950, the GI Forum passed a resolution criticizing the then senator Lyndon B. Johnson of Texas for siding with growers who wanted to reduce federal funding for detention camps and airlifts of deported illegal workers to Mexico:

> Whereas Senator Johnson owes in large measure his position in the U.S. Senate to the votes of thousands of citizens of Mexican descent in South Texas . . . and whereas Senator Johnson's actions have been contributing to the principles of liberalism expounded by the late Franklin Delano Roosevelt . . . [h]is vote [against more funding for detention and deportation of illegal immigrant workers] is in utter disregard of the friendship in which he has been held by thousands of citizens of Mexican descent.[9]

The subsequent abolition during Johnson's presidency in 1964 of the Bracero program, an exploitative Mexican guest-worker program used by southwestern agribusiness, was supported by Mexican American leaders, labor unions, and New Deal liberals.

Cesar Chavez, who cofounded the United Farm Workers (UFW) in 1962 with Dolores Huerta, denounced illegal immigration and reported unauthorized migrant workers to the Border Patrol. In 1974, Chavez explained his position: "The illegal aliens are doubly exploited, first because they are farm workers, and second because they are powerless to defend their own interests. But if there were no illegals being used to break our strikes, we could win those strikes overnight and then be in a position to improve the living and working conditions of all farm workers."[10] Chavez supported an amnesty for some illegal immigrants to prevent divide-and-rule tactics by employers.

Had the United Farm Workers succeeded in organizing more than two million farmworkers, it would have been one of the largest private sector labor unions in the United States.[11] As one study in 2010 notes, "Unions, primarily the UFW and the Teamsters, had their maximum impacts on farm wages and benefits between the mid-1960s and the early 1980s, a period of very low immigration. The Bracero program ended in 1964, and unauthorized migration did not begin to surge until 1983, when a then-record 1.3 million foreigners were apprehended by the Border Patrol (peak apprehension years were 1986 and 2000, with 1.8 million each year)."

But the efforts of Chavez and his allies on behalf of farmworkers were in vain. American agribusiness employers succeeded in using cross-border labor arbitrage to defeat the UFW. By 2021, nearly half of U.S. farmworkers were illegal immigrants, most of them from Mexico or Central America.[12]

The economist Giovanni Peri is one of the experts most frequently cited by progressive and libertarian advocates of increased immigration. In 2007, in "How Immigrants Affect

California Employment and Wages," a policy brief for the Public Policy Institute of California, Peri declared, "First, there is no evidence that the inflow of immigrants over the period 1960–2004 worsened the employment opportunities of natives with similar education and experience."[13]

Peri's statement is demonstrably false. To name one of many examples of empirical studies of the subject, a 1988 study by the General Accounting Office reviewed the empirical (not theoretical) academic literature and identified numerous cases in which employers had recently substituted illegal immigrants, most of them from Mexico, for American workers or legal immigrants.[14] Many of these examples came from California.

Shoe workers: "In the 1940s the Southern California industry paid the highest wages in the nation for comparable workers. . . . International migrants (many of whom are illegal) represent most of the supply of skilled shoe workers in Los Angeles and put downward pressure on wages and working conditions."[15]

Restaurant workers in Los Angeles: "In the study, 37 out of 52 surveyed restaurant managers believed that international migrants either held down wages or averted a labor shortage for kitchen workers. Thirty-nine of these employers admitted to having replaced native workers (Mexican-Americans, Blacks, and Anglos) with Spanish-speaking international migrants."[16]

Citrus pickers: "In Ventura County citrus, a group of settled mostly legal workers gained increases in wages and benefits during the 1970s. In the 1975 to 1985 period, farm labor contractors using more recently arrived international migrants, the majority of whom were illegal, were able to drive down compensation by at least 18 percent for citrus pickers in the area."[17]

Tomato workers: "In San Diego County legal tomato workers lost their jobs or accepted a substantial cut in pay during the 1970s as growers shifted to the greater use of illegal workers. . . . Wage rates were above $4.00 an hour and some growers had signed contracts with the United Farm Workers (UFW) which included health benefits and a pension plan. By the late 1970s, however, North County growers were able to reduce labor costs to $3.35 an hour."[18]

Janitors: "In the post–World War II period, the janitors working in the high-rise districts of Los Angeles, about half of whom were U.S. blacks, had won excellent wages and working conditions under the leadership of the Service Employees International Union (SEIU). But, in the early 1980s a group of aggressive non-union firms, who hired predominantly illegal workers, were able to wrest the best building contracts from the unionized firms. As a result, wages fell and most of the U.S.-born black janitors lost their jobs."[19]

The use of both legal and illegal immigrants as strikebreakers and replacement workers by employers continues in our time. Here is Natalie Kitroeff in the *Los Angeles Times* in 2017: "Immigrants Flooded California Construction. Worker Pay Sank. Here's Why."[20] Another journalist, Sara Murray, wrote about the destruction of unions in the U.S. meatpacking industry for *The Wall Street Journal* in 2013: "On the Killing Floor, Clues to the Impact of Immigration on Jobs."[21]

At the high end of the wage scale in the United States, Silicon Valley tech companies and Wall Street firms and other businesses have become addicted to a steady supply of college-educated H-1B indentured servants from overseas. Companies like Google, Apple, Microsoft, and JPMorgan hire H-1Bs directly or rent these guest workers from contractors known as body shops, many of them Indian firms, like Tata Consultancy Services.

The H-1B program employs relatively few workers in the United States, but they form a disproportionate share of the workforce in the tech "jobs of the future" touted by American business leaders, politicians, and pundits. Between 1980 and 2010, chiefly as a result of the massive expansion of the H-1B program, the number of American computer science jobs held by foreign-born workers exploded from 7.1 percent to 27.8 percent.

In 2020, 74.1 percent of the 407,071 H-1B visas issued to specialty foreign workers by the United States went to nationals from India.[22] The idea that three-quarters of the workers on earth outside U.S. borders who possess valuable skills desperately needed by Silicon Valley and Wall Street and other U.S. industries just happen to live in one country is obviously absurd. The predominance of young Indian men among H-1Bs merely reflects the accidental importance of Indian "body shops" as suppliers of indentured servants to U.S. companies beginning in the 1990s.

From its earliest days, the United States has benefited from workers with particular skills that do not exist in this country—British textile mill workers in the nineteenth century, Welsh ironmongers in the infant U.S. steel industry, and German rocket scientists like Krafft Ehricke and Wernher von Braun during the space age after World War II. But most H-1Bs, even though they are defined as "specialty workers," have no unique skills that are not shared with U.S. graduates of STEM programs.[23]

According to the American Immigration Council, an advocacy group that does not disclose its donors on its web page, "Research shows that H-1B workers complement U.S. workers, fill employment gaps in many STEM occupations, and expand job opportunities for all." This would come as news to the many Americans, like a number of workers at Disney, who have been fired by U.S. companies after being forced to train the H-1B indentured servants who replaced them.[24] These and other cases raise an obvious question: If H-1B guest workers are so skilled, why do they need to be trained by the American workers whom they replace?

If there were really a shortage of skilled workers, one would expect Silicon Valley firms to lobby Congress for a points system like those of Canada, Australia, and the U.K. Such a merit system would favor skilled immigrants and assign them points based on their English proficiency, education, particular skills, and so on. Instead, through front groups like FWD.us, launched with the help of Facebook's cofounder Mark Zuckerberg in 2013, major tech corporations and others constantly lobby Congress to expand the H-1B visa numbers.

Why don't the CEOs of Apple, Facebook, Google, Intel, and

other tech companies agitate for a merit-based system to select skilled immigrants? There are two reasons: employer profits and employer power.

We can start with tech company profits. Under a points-based merit system, tech companies would lose the savings on wage costs that are created by labor arbitrage that exploits the difference between what H-1B indentured servants are paid and what most American citizens and green card holders would demand as pay for the same jobs, in the absence of the H-1B program.

The U.S. Department of Labor sets four H-1B wage levels, based on the median wage of other workers in the same occupation and region, with the help of data from the Occupational Employment and Wage Statistics survey by the Bureau of Labor Statistics. This system is supposed to protect American workers and legal permanent residents from having their wages undercut by competition with H-1Bs. But as Daniel Costa and Ron Hira point out in a 2020 study, the Department of Labor sets the two lowest wage levels for H-1Bs well below the local median wage.

"Not surprisingly," Costa and Hira write, "three-fifths of all H-1B jobs were certified at the two lowest prevailing wage levels in 2019." Among the top employers of H-1Bs, IBM had three-fifths of its H-1B workers assigned to Level 1 or Level 2, Amazon and Microsoft had three-quarters each, Google had more than half, and Walmart and Uber had roughly half each. If H-1Bs are geniuses with unique and valuable skills that both American workers and immigrants with green cards lack, then why are tech firms and their contractors so careful to pay most of their H-1Bs the very lowest wages permissible under U.S. law? Costa and Hira conclude: "Wage-level data make clear that most H-1B employers—but especially the biggest users, by nature of the sheer volume of workers they employ—are taking advantage of a flawed H-1B prevailing wage rule to underpay their workers relative to market wage standards, resulting in major savings in labor costs for companies that use the H-1B."[25]

But there is more than considerations of profit in the preference of the managers and shareholders of U.S. tech firms like Apple, Microsoft, Google, and Facebook for noncitizen indentured servants over free labor. A merit-based points system would allow skilled immigrants to work for any firm they chose, but *indentured servants are bound to their sponsors—corporations and body shops.* The most fundamental right of a free worker—the right to quit and take another job in the same country, without the employer's permission—is denied to H-1B workers, making them more easily intimidated by their employers and afraid to complain about abuses. Employers' preference for workers with little or no workplace bargaining power, quite apart from considerations of labor costs, explains their lobbying to expand the number of indentured servants as well as their hostility to organized labor.

Like defenders of corporate offshoring policies, defenders of immigration labor arbitrage often claim that the harm, if there is any, affects only a few workers, whose personal suffering is outweighed by the benefits to the economy as a whole and consumers.

A frequent argument of the corporate- and billionaire-funded mass immigration lobby is that immigrants increase gross domestic product (GDP) and create new jobs in the United States. Inasmuch as GDP increases as the labor force increases, this is true, but irrelevant. In terms of long-term national prosperity, what counts is not gross GDP, or even GDP per capita, but per capita productivity. If the addition of immigrant workers reduces the incentive of employers to invest in laborsaving technology, then more immigration will mean lower productivity growth and lower long-term prosperity, compared with other, more mechanized and automated societies.

A related argument for mass immigration is that by their very presence in a country immigrants as consumers create jobs for natives and other immigrants. But the specific kinds of jobs that are generated by immigrants as consumers depend on their incomes. Increase the number of impoverished immigrants in America and you will increase the number of low-rent apartments, discount stores, coin-operated laundries used by people too poor to purchase washers and dryers for their homes, and payday lenders charging usurious interest rates to poor people who lack bank accounts.

In addition to expanding the sorts of businesses that prey on the poor, mass low-wage immigration creates jobs in government welfare bureaucracies and religious and secular nonprofits that are contractors to the welfare bureaucracy, because immigrants in the United States are more likely than U.S. natives to depend on public assistance. According to the National Academies of Sciences Engineering, and Medicine, in 2011 19.9 percent of immigrants and 32.1 percent of the children of immigrants under 18 lived in poverty, compared with 13.5 percent of native-born citizens.[26] In another report, the National Academies found that 45 percent of immigrant households relied on welfare assistance for food and 46 percent on Medicaid.[27]

Growth in low-rent apartments, discount stores, and welfare bureaucracies is indeed economic growth as a result of low-wage immigration, but is it the kind of growth that any developed nation should seek to promote?

Some leftists and libertarians argue that allowing mass immigration to developed countries will help poor nations develop. But the math does not work. In 2019, the foreign-born share of the U.S. population was 13.7 percent and the foreign-born share of the U.S. workforce was 17.2 percent, having risen from 6.2 percent and 6.7 percent in 1980, at the end of the New Deal era and the beginning of the neoliberal era in the United States.[28] But in 2020 only 3.6 percent of the world's population were international migrants, living outside their countries of origin, with nearly two-thirds of them living in high-income countries like the United States, Canada, and European nations.[29] While many of these individual immigrants no doubt improved their conditions by moving, the remaining 96 percent of the human race experienced no personal benefits.

What about remittances—the money that immigrants send

to family or spend in their home countries? While remittances from emigrants are large as a share of national GDP in a few countries that are extremely tiny (38.98 percent in the case of Tonga, with a population of 105,697 in 2020) or extremely poor (24.91 percent in the case of Somalia), for low-income countries in general remittances from the country's emigrants abroad contribute no more than around 4 percent of GDP, as in Nigeria (3.98 percent of GDP) and in Mexico (3.94 percent).[30] No country has ever joined the ranks of developed industrial economies on the basis of remittances from the impoverished workers it sends to the low-wage labor markets of industrialized countries.

Are there jobs that Americans refuse to do, as the cheap-labor right and the open-borders left both insist? No. Non-immigrants work in large numbers in almost all of the occupations in which immigrants are concentrated. In 2014, illegal immigrants made up an estimated 5 percent of the U.S. workforce (given the lack of data and widespread forgery of identity credentials, the number could be higher or lower). They were around a fifth or more in the following industries: dry cleaning and laundry (18 percent), building maintenance (19 percent), apparel manufacturing (19 percent), landscaping (21 percent), private household employment (22 percent), and crop production (22 percent).[31] In all food jobs—ranging from production to distribution and retail—legal and illegal immigrant workers combined were no more than 23 percent of the workforce in total, reaching a maximum of 30 percent in food production.[32]

When farmers, ranchers, home builders, and others complain

that they can't find enough American workers, what they really mean is they cannot find enough Americans willing to *work for the wages they prefer to pay.* Unless wages are skyrocketing in a particular occupation or industry, the claim by employers in that sector that there is a labor shortage is obviously false.

Defenders of both global labor arbitrage and immigration labor arbitrage at the expense of American worker power and national productivity growth make similar appeals to the well-being of American consumers who buy goods and services made by workers paid low wages, here or abroad. Like the benefits of offshoring to consumers, the benefits of low-wage immigration to the United States are enormously exaggerated by employer lobbies and their mouthpieces in the media and government.

In 1997, an expert panel of the National Research Council of the National Academy of Sciences concluded that competition with unskilled immigrants explained nearly half of the decline in wages between 1980 and 1994 for native-born high school dropouts, who were disproportionately black and Hispanic.[33] At the same time, the National Research Council estimated that the annual economy-wide benefit from immigration could be no more than $18 billion (about $32 billion in 2022) in an economy of roughly $23 *trillion.*[34] And even that minuscule economic benefit, at the cost of a significant wage decline for the least skilled American workers, would go disproportionately to the affluent American individuals and businesses who are most likely to employ low-wage immigrants as workers, servants, or service vendors.

This raises an obvious question: If lowering the prices of goods and services by lowering the wages of the workers who provide them is such a good idea, then why not help American consumers even more by lowering the wages of all American workers, not merely those who compete with foreign workers or immigrants? Instead of raising the minimum wage, why not lower it or abolish it altogether? Why not legalize child labor in the United States? Consumers would benefit from lower prices!

To argue against low-wage immigration is not to argue against immigration as such. Immigration policy as a whole is made up of different policies with different goals, including refugee policy, family policy, and the recruitment of rare individuals with truly scarce and valuable skills. People of goodwill can disagree about particular categories and quantities of immigration. My point in this chapter is that for several generations U.S. immigration policy has been weaponized by American employers, as one of a number of instruments, along with union busting, outsourcing, anti-worker labor laws, and the offshoring of production, that are used to undermine the bargaining power of American workers and their ability to demand higher wages, better benefits, and better working conditions.

The success of the employer offensive on multiple fronts against American worker bargaining power in the twenty-first-century United States has created a class of "the working poor"—full-time workers who are unable to support themselves and their families on their wages and depend on government welfare to survive. How the pro-employer welfare state in the United States subsidizes low-wage employers, how Americans seek to escape being trapped in low-wage occupations by obtaining college diplomas or occupational licenses, and how the frantic credential arms race warps American society in areas from family formation to partisan politics are the subjects of the next few chapters.

CHAPTER SIX

Scrooge Revisited

The Anti-worker Welfare State

In previous chapters, we saw how American employers have used a variety of strategies to lower the wages of American workers: nearly annihilating organized labor in the private sector workforce, reclassifying and outsourcing jobs to lower wage and benefit costs, and taking advantage of global labor arbitrage to replace more-expensive American workers with less-expensive foreign workers, including legal immigrants, illegal immigrants, and indentured servants ("guest workers"). The campaign of American employer lobbies over the last half century has succeeded in its goal of lowering wages or preventing wages from rising to the levels to which they might have grown absent the destruction of worker bargaining power.

But the success of the half-century employer offensive against

American worker power has produced a problem: Who will take care of the growing number of workers who cannot survive, as individuals or as family heads, on the paltry wages that they are paid? Americans are too generous to allow workers and their families to starve to death because they are paid starvation wages. The American welfare state keeps underpaid workers alive, with American taxpayers picking up the bill.

Adam Smith took it for granted that workers should be paid not only a living wage but also a family wage, sufficient to pay for all of the living costs of the children as well as the parents:

> A man must always live by his work, and his wages must at least be sufficient to maintain him. They must even upon most occasions be somewhat more, otherwise it would be impossible for him to bring up a family, and the race of such workmen could not last beyond the first generation.[1]

Even in the case of a two-earner couple, Smith wrote, the husband and wife needed to be paid much more than was necessary for themselves alone so that they could meet the costs of raising children: "Thus far at least seems certain, that, in order to bring up a family, the labour of the husband and wife together must, even in the lowest species of common labour, be able to earn something more than what is precisely necessary for their own maintenance."[2]

If wages were too low, Smith worried that workers would not be able to support themselves as individuals, much less support their families. The result of excessively low wages would be social turmoil:

> The lowest class being not only overstocked with its own workmen, but with the overflowing of all the other classes, the competition for employment would be so great in it, as to reduce the wages of labor to the most miserable and scanty subsistence of the laborer. Many would either starve, or be driven to seek a subsistence either by begging, or by the perpetration perhaps of the greatest enormities.[3]

As an alternative to starvation, begging, crime, and revolt, a rudimentary welfare state had existed for centuries in Britain in the form of the Poor Laws. Smith denounced the punitive nature of the poverty relief system of his day: "There is scarce a poor man in England of forty years of age, I will venture to say, who has not in some part of his life felt himself most cruelly oppressed by this ill-contrived law."[4] None of these evils would exist, Smith believed, if employers paid adequate wages.

Unlike Adam Smith, Ebenezer Scrooge, the fictitious Victorian-era British capitalist who is the protagonist of Charles Dickens's story *A Christmas Carol*, had no objection to paying taxes or making philanthropic donations to support a minimal, punitive, pro-employer welfare state—the nineteenth-century British Poor Law, with its treadmills and workhouses—along with prisons for the poor who turned to crime. For Scrooge, as for modern neo-liberals and libertarians and free-market conservatives, the alternative of requiring all employers to pay every worker a living wage was unthinkable. If an employer chooses not to pay a living wage, that is a problem for the employee and the public, not the employer.

In *A Christmas Carol*, Dickens includes a scene in which Scrooge is approached during the Christmas season by several philanthropists trying to raise money for charity:

> "At this festive season of the year, Mr. Scrooge . . . it is more than usually desirable that we should make some slight provision for the poor and destitute, who suffer greatly at the present time. Many thousands are in want of common necessaries; hundreds of thousands are in want of common comforts, sir."
>
> "Are there no prisons?" asked Scrooge.
>
> "Plenty of prisons," said the gentleman, laying down the pen again.
>
> "And the Union workhouses?" demanded Scrooge. "Are they still in operation?"
>
> "They are. Still," returned the gentleman, "I wish I could say they were not."
>
> "The Treadmill and the Poor Law are in full vigour, then?" said Scrooge.

"Both very busy, sir."

"Oh! I was afraid, from what you said at first, that something had occurred to stop them in their useful course," said Scrooge. "I'm very glad to hear it. . . . I help to support the establishments I have mentioned: they cost enough: and those who are badly off must go there."[5]

Adam Smith and Ebenezer Scrooge symbolize the two basic approaches to organizing a modern industrial society in which most production is privately owned and the vast majority of people must earn a living by selling their labor to private employers for wages, if we reject a socialist system, democratic or authoritarian, that unites political and economic power in the hands of a single elite. One approach is to ensure that all full-time workers get wages that are adequate to pay not only for the recurring costs of themselves and their families but also for their savings and their contributions to insurance, including compulsory government social insurance against poverty in old age. In this system, the only people who need to rely on means-tested public assistance—"welfare"—are those who cannot work and are not eligible for other kinds of insurance, including social insurance based on a history of payroll tax contributions. Nobody who works full time should be poor. We can call this system the living-wage/social-insurance model.

The other way to structure a market economy with a majority of wage earners is the low-wage/high-welfare model. By "high welfare" I do not mean generous universal benefit programs in the sense of the post-1945 Nordic welfare states. I mean instead that public assistance, which can take the form of cash or in-kind subsidies like food stamps and public housing in the United States, accounts for a high proportion of the total income of a low-wage worker, when welfare and the wage paid by the employer are added together.

In the last century, the United States has used both of these models for organizing a society of wage earners, for roughly half a century in each case. The New Deal order, from the 1930s to the 1980s, was a version of a living-wage/social-insurance system. The neoliberal order from the 1950s to the 1980s is based on the low-wage/high-welfare system.

Contrary to the mythology shared by many contemporary American progressives and conservatives, the half-century New Deal regime under Democratic presidents like Franklin Delano Roosevelt and Lyndon B. Johnson and the Republican presidents Dwight Eisenhower and Richard Nixon was not characterized by high levels of redistribution from rich to poor. Living wages meant that few full-time workers needed means-tested public assistance or "welfare." Living wages also ensured the solvency of the universal, contributory, work-based social-insurance system that included unemployment insurance and Social Security. Social insurance was paid for out of flat payroll taxes on all wage income up to a point, rather than high progressive taxes on the rich. This funding model reflects the nature of social insurance as government-brokered mutual insurance among workers rather than redistribution from rich to poor. (In practice, a degree of redistribution within Social Security and other social-insurance programs ameliorates the regressive nature of flat payroll taxes.)

Public assistance or "welfare," with eligibility limited to the poor, was intended by mid-century American policy makers to be accessible only to those who could not or should not work through no fault of their own, including the disabled and the widowed mothers of young children, who most Americans of the time believed should not be in the labor market. In his 1935 State of the Union address, President Roosevelt declared that cash relief to adults capable of working and without child-care duties was "a narcotic, a subtle destroyer of the human spirit," to which the alternative should be a public job with a living wage, if no living-wage private jobs were available.

Since the 1980s, the New Deal's living-wage/low-welfare system has been replaced by the low-wage/high-welfare system of neoliberal America. Today in the United States employers are allowed to pay poverty wages—wages too low for millions of workers and their families to live on. To make up the gap between what workers earn and what their families need to survive, the American taxpayer has been forced to pay the bill.

Even in 2018, as the economy was recovering from the Great Recession, 12 percent of the seventy-nine million families in the United States had received Supplemental Nutrition Assistance Program benefits or "food stamps" at least once in the previous year. Of these families, 79 percent included at least one worker, and nearly half of married-couple families on food stamps had two workers.[6] In 2020, according to the Government Accountability Office, 70 percent of adult workers who took part in the Medicaid and food stamps programs worked full time.[7]

In the United States, fast-food workers are more than twice as likely to rely on public welfare programs to survive as the American workforce in general, at 52 percent compared with 25 percent, according to a study by scholars at the University of California at Berkeley in 2013. The fact that a quarter of the entire American workforce in the twenty-first century was so poorly paid that it needed to rely on one or another means-tested welfare program would have shocked mid-twentieth-century Roosevelt Democrats and Eisenhower Republicans.[8]

Walmart, America's largest chain store, was the center of controversy in 2014 because the wages it paid many of its workers were so low that they could not survive without using public welfare programs. Americans for Tax Fairness estimated that the American taxpayer paid $6.2 billion to low-wage Walmart employees who had to supplement their meager earnings with food stamps, housing vouchers for the poor, and the means-tested Medicaid program of public health insurance for low-income Americans.[9] Around the same time, the National Employment Law Project found that 60 percent of the $7 billion in annual welfare benefits that went to low-wage workers went to the employees of only ten corporations, with McDonald's alone responsible for $1.2 billion.[10]

In 2018, Senator Bernie Sanders, the independent socialist

from Vermont who ran for the Democratic nomination for president in 2016 and 2020, and Representative Ro Khanna (D-Calif.) introduced the Stop Bad Employers by Zeroing Out Subsidies (BEZOS) Act, whose acronym was a play on the name of Jeff Bezos, the founder and owner of Amazon who has fought unionization of Amazon warehouses. Under the bill, corporations would have to pay a tax in the amount of the means-tested public assistance that all of their employers received. The Labor Center of the University of California at Berkeley has calculated that welfare for low-wage American workers costs taxpayers $150 billion each year.[11]

Just how large what might be called the "welfare wage" can be compared to the low market wage that it supplements is illustrated by a striking example from the state of New York. In 2016, a single full-time worker with two children working for the New York State minimum wage of $9 an hour would have had an annual income of $18,720. On an annual basis, the same worker would have been eligible for federal earned income tax credit (EITC) of $5,513, a separate New York state EITC of $1,654, a New York City EITC of $276, SNAP benefits (food stamps) of $6,132, a federal child tax credit of $2,000, and a state-level Empire Child Tax Credit of $660. These public wage subsidies and welfare benefits add up to $16,235—nearly 87 percent of the worker's market pay. An annual market wage that equaled the combination of the minimum wage and the various government subsidies in this case, assuming fifty weeks of forty-hour work per year and two weeks of paid vacation time, would be $34,955, or $16.80 per hour. That is hardly an exorbitant salary for a full-time worker in New York City, and the hourly wage is near the minimum wage target of the "Fight for $15" campaign. Instead of requiring that the employer pay the hypothetical worker a living wage, however, the U.S. federal government, the New York state government, and the city of New York in this example together allow the employer to pay only $9 an hour and send the bill for nearly half of the worker's expenses to those who pay federal, state, and city taxes.[12]

The neoliberal deal is terrible for workers and taxpayers. But it is great for employers, who are enabled to pay low wages by the welfare state.

As the example of the British Poor Law demonstrates, a welfare state can be pro-worker or pro-employer, depending on how it is designed.

From an amoral, antisocial, and rational employer's perspective, the ultimate pro-employer welfare state would be one that combines miserly, means-tested social assistance for workers with requirements that the same workers must work for low wages before they can access various welfare programs. This system serves the employer of cheap labor very well. The taxpayers who pay for the welfare programs enable the employer to pay wages too low for workers to live on. At the same time, the decision of government to keep the means-tested benefits low increases pressure on welfare recipients to take bad jobs with low wages. Poor workers must supplement scanty benefits with low pay and supplement low pay with scanty benefits. And by forcing people who need welfare to take any available jobs, usually low-wage jobs, in order to receive their paltry benefits, the government also supplies the employer with a pool of desperate workers who will accept the poverty wages that are offered, a pool of workers who are unlikely to protest against abuses, for fear that their public benefits will be cut off. The low-wage/high-welfare economy is a vicious circle.

Of every welfare state program—whether universal social insurance or means-tested social assistance for the poor only—the same question can be asked: Does this program increase or reduce the bargaining power of workers in negotiations with employers? Unemployment insurance is an example. The longer the period of unemployment insurance lasts, the choosier unemployed people can be about their next jobs, waiting to find one with higher wages and better benefits rather than settling for the first inferior job that is offered. An unemployment insurance system designed to benefit employers, in contrast, will provide benefits as briefly as possible so that the cutoff of the insurance quickly forces workers to take any jobs available on the terms offered by employers, no matter how miserable.

What the political scientist Jacob Hacker calls the "great risk shift" is another way in which employers privatize the benefits that come from their employment of workers while socializing the costs.[13] For example, in the last half century most U.S. employers have replaced employer pensions, which put the risk of future payment on the employers, with either no pensions or defined-contribution pensions like 401(k)s, which transfer the risk of losing money in retirement from employers to individual workers.

A wage subsidy that goes only to poorly paid workers is perhaps the most blatant example of pro-employer welfare. One of the largest antipoverty programs in the United States is the wage subsidy known as the earned income tax credit. Working parents with children, and some working individuals, are eligible for the federal EITC; there are supplementary state EITCs as well.

The EITC is successful in reducing poverty among low-income workers. In 2018, it is estimated to have raised 16.5 million Americans, including 3 million children, out of poverty.[14] But like all wage subsidies, it enables many employers to pay poverty wages too low for their workers to live on without the government money. As Teresa Ghilarducci and Aida Farmand note, "The heavy reliance on the EITC, rather than the minimum wage and the strength of trade unions, is one major reason why the United States leads the OECD in the share of jobs that pay poverty wages—a full 25.3 percent of jobs are poverty jobs, compared to 3 percent of jobs in Norway." Supporting the intuition that subsidizing low-wage jobs creates more of them and suppresses wage growth is the fact that states that lack a state EITC or have only a small one in addition to the federal EITC have shown higher wage growth than the "generous" states.[15]

Child-care policy is perhaps the most dramatic example of a welfare state program that can either strengthen or weaken the bargaining power of workers and their families relative to employers. Systems of child-care support in other industrial democracies tend to fall into two categories: general family support and dual-earner support.

General family support policies, found in many continental European countries influenced by Catholic pro-natalism, typically take the form of cash subsidies that can be used either to purchase paid day care outside the home or to defray the living expenses of a stay-at-home mother or other caregiver. The Canadian system of general family support, created by pro-family Canadian conservatives, provides parents with cash allowances that they are free to use either to support a family caregiver or to pay outsiders for child care.

The dual-earner family support approach takes the form of government subsidies for public day-care services from birth onward. The dual-earner model is dominant in the Nordic countries: Sweden, Norway, Denmark, and Finland.[16] The dual-earner model is promoted by those on the socialist and radical feminist left who seek the "defamilization" of the welfare state through the socialization of child care, on the theory that maternal care is a relic of patriarchy or the bourgeois capitalist economy.

If a national referendum were held in the United States today,

there is little doubt that the flexible Canadian model of cash subsidies to families, including both two-earner and one-earner families, would prevail over a Swedish-style model that promotes a
two-earner family ideal by subsidizing institutional providers of
child care but not parental caregivers. Even in 2018, only a slight
majority (55 percent) of American mothers were employed full
time, with 17 percent employed part time or caring for children
at home (28 percent).[17] According to a 2019 Gallup poll, mothers
of children under eighteen who "prefer to stay at home and take
care of the house and family" outnumber those who prefer to work
by 50 percent to 45 percent.[18] A Pew poll in the same year found
that among all Americans only 33 percent think that working full
time is the ideal situation for mothers with young children; the
rest are divided between those who think that mothers should not
work while their children are young (21 percent) and those who
think that part-time work is appropriate (42 percent).[19]

In 2021, American Compass, a heterodox think tank, asked respondents to identify themselves by class: lower, working, middle, and upper (households with more than $150,000 in annual
income). Majorities of lower-class and working-class families opted
for "one adult working full time, one adult not working," while
the middle class (slightly) and the upper class (by a huge margin)
opted for "two adults working full time." When asked about the
preferred arrangement of couples with children under five years
of age, the middle class deserted the upper class and joined the
income classes below it.[20]

Although the general family support model is more popular

among Americans than the dual-earner model, it makes sense for selfish employer lobbies to oppose flexible child-care subsidies that would enable millions of parental caregivers, mostly but not exclusively mothers, to voluntarily withdraw wholly or partly from the labor market. That withdrawal would tighten labor markets and increase the bargaining power of the workers who remained, increasing pressure on employers to raise wages and improve working conditions.

Because those who care for young children at home are usually their mothers or other female relatives, the subject is often discussed in terms of "female labor force participation," which is treated as something good in itself by employer lobbies and their political allies. It is easier for businesses to boost output simply by maximizing the number of workers in the workforce than it is to invest in laborsaving technology to boost per capita labor productivity. The alliance between business interests and defamilizing feminist radicals explains why the neoliberal Democratic Party in Congress under President Joe Biden, proposing government funding for day-care centers, rejected the option of giving parents flexible benefits that they could choose to use to pay for outside public or private day care or for a caregiver at home.

Here is Gina Raimondo, U.S. secretary of commerce, in an op-ed in 2021 stating what is usually left unspoken—the consensus in American elite circles that every mother should be in the workforce, in order to boost profits and GDP growth: "Even before COVID-19, the lack of child care cost Americans $37 billion annually in lost income and $13 billion in lost productivity and employees. Without adequate care services, *we cannot expect everyone who is a parent or caregiver to fully participate in the workforce* [emphasis added]." Raimondo continues: "I've spoken with dozens of CEOs. They recognize the return on investment. At a recent event, Dara Khosrowshahi told me how turnover at Uber, often caused by caregiving demands, costs $4,000 in lost productivity per employee."[21] (Uber's business model, it should be noted, is based on the transportation company's legal claim that its drivers are independent contractors, so that many costs are shifted to them and so that many labor laws protecting employees do not apply.)

Defamilizing welfare state reforms implicitly treat the two-parent, one-earner family as patriarchal, oppressive, illegitimate, outmoded, and bad for the bottom line of American corporations. The Biden administration's fact sheet explaining the American Families Plan contains passages that sound as if they were written by labor-hungry employer lobbies: "In part due to the lack of [two-earner] family friendly policies, the United States has fallen behind its competitors in female labor force participation." The administration goes so far as to claim that the United States suffers from a day-care gap in the new cold war competition with China: "Together, these plans reinvest in the future of the American economy and American workers, and will help us out-compete China and other countries around the world."[22]

Stay-at-home moms lower U.S. GDP by lowering female workforce participation! Parental caregivers are fifth columnists for China, which seeks to undermine the U.S. economy! Citizens, if you see any parents instead of paid caregivers in the presence of small children at home between the hours of 8:00 a.m. and 5:00 p.m., report the slackers to the authorities immediately!

The alliance between the defamilizing left and employer lobbies explains why Sweden adopted the dual-earner model in childcare policy, rather than the general family support model. The golden age of Swedish social democracy, when the small Nordic country enjoyed high wages, high productivity, and high equality, was known as the housewife era and rested on the male breadwinner/female caregiver model, like New Deal America. Defamilizing feminism in Swedish public policy emerged as the social democratic model began to break down in the 1970s. It was only then that Sweden built its enormous and expensive public daycare system—with the support of Swedish employers, according to one scholar: "Decisions were made to expand women's labor supply, rather than bring in guest workers to cope with labor shortages, as in the continental European countries, or to ease immigration policies, as in the United States."[23]

Like Ebenezer Scrooge, employers in the United States do not oppose the welfare state, as long as the rules of the welfare state are written in their favor. Complementing and reinforcing America's low-wage, low-worker-power institutional regime, the American welfare state, it is worth repeating, privatizes the benefits of cheap labor and socializes the costs.

CHAPTER SEVEN

The Credential Arms Race

In 1985, according to the Cost-of-Thriving Index developed by Oren Cass of American Compass, a typical male American worker could pay for the housing, health care, transportation, and education of a family of four on thirty weeks of salary, while it took fifty-three weeks to do so in 2018.[1] Between 1985 and 2020, the number of weeks needed for a typical female American worker to cover basic expenses rose from forty-five to sixty-six.[2]

Critics of comparisons like this argue that many contemporary working-class Americans can afford sophisticated gadgets like iPhones and big-screen TVs, even if they cannot afford home ownership and are vulnerable to medical bankruptcy. What is not in dispute is the fact that, because of the collapse of organized labor and the bargaining power of wage earners in general, ladders from the working class to the middle class for Americans with no more than a high school education have crumbled.

With few exceptions, in the early twenty-first century what was considered a generic middle-class lifestyle half a century ago is a luxury limited to managers, professionals, and some remaining small business owners and self-employed workers. Access to those favored occupations in our time almost always requires a credential that is expensive in terms of money, time, or both— one or more university diplomas or an occupational license.

The correlation in the last half century between the decline of private sector unionization and the massive expansion of college degrees and occupational licensing requirements is apparent. The inverse correlation is particularly striking in the case of college diplomas. In 1960, 31.9 percent of private sector workers were unionized, and only 7.7 percent of Americans had college degrees.[3] In 2019, only 6.2 percent of Americans in the private sector were unionized, and 37.5 percent had college degrees.[4] The two trends are mirror images.

The same pattern is evident in the spread of occupational licensing. In the 1950s, when a third of the private sector workforce was unionized, only a tenth of the workforce required licenses to be eligible to work at their jobs. Today a quarter of American workers must have occupational licenses.[5]

Both kinds of credentialism produce wage premiums for workers comparable to the union wage premium. Between 1979 and 2013, the average worker between the ages of twenty-five and sixty-four with a college degree or more went from earning around 35 percent more than a high-school-educated worker to earning 80 percent more.[6]

Meanwhile, holders of occupational licenses enjoy a 15 percent wage premium over similar unlicensed workers.[7] Compare this with a recent estimation of the union wage premium of 10.2 percent in the United States.[8] The economists Morris M. Kleiner and Alan B. Krueger suggest that workers have pushed for occupational licensing in part to counteract the decline in worker power that has resulted from the destruction of private sector unions in the United States. They conclude that "the wage premium associated with licensing is strikingly similar to that found in studies of the effect of unions on wages."[9]

While the possession of credentials can compensate for the absence of union membership in the case of individual workers, the effects on the workforce and society in general of credentialism and unionism are quite different. Unions tend to benefit non-unionized workers in several ways. One is "union threat." The mere possibility that employees will demand that a non-union firm be unionized can lead employers to raise wages, provide benefits, or otherwise improve job conditions, in the hope that more contented workers will not seek to join a union.

The presence of unions can help non-union workers in another way. If workers quit non-union jobs to take jobs with unionized firms or firms with other kinds of collective bargaining coverage, the non-union employers may be forced to raise wages and benefits to compete with the unionized employers. The importance of the "union threat" phenomenon was evident in 2022, when, following the first example of unionization of an Amazon warehouse, Amazon announced it would raise hourly wages for warehouse workers and delivery drivers, as well as provide new benefits, including allowing workers flexible access to up to 70 percent of their pay during a month without fees.[10]

Licensing, like unionization, benefits workers, but without positive effects on non-licensed workers comparable to the positive effects of unions on non-union workers. Educational or licensing requirements shrink the number of people who are qualified to practice a profession or trade, artificially creating tight labor markets in that occupation and allowing credentialed insiders to charge customers or employers more for their services. It is in the interest of the credentialed insiders to make the barriers to entry to their occupation as high as possible, to keep the number of their competitors low and the occupational labor market tight. It is not surprising, therefore, that both kinds of credentials—diplomas and occupational licenses—tend to require programs of education that are far more complex and time-consuming than the typical practice of the trade requires. The complexity and prolonged time may not be necessary to be successful in the field, but they succeed at weeding out many potential rivals who give up and drop out before completing the training.[11]

The "liberal professions" in the United States and other English-speaking countries—law, medicine, university teaching, and the clergy—were not traditionally called "liberal" because their practitioners were mostly on the political left (though nowadays they are). "Liberal" derives from a Latin word that meant suitable to a member of the tiny free-citizen elite, in a society in which most people were slaves or mechanics. The liberal occupations were liberal because they combined high status and good pay and were therefore appropriate for the children of the bourgeoisie and aristocracy. At the same time, the liberal professions were artisanal, in the sense that their practitioners were generalists who were often self-employed, like blacksmiths or cobblers, but with much higher prestige and incomes.

In the modern industrial era, the members of the liberal professions have fought desperately against two threats to their high social status and autonomy. The first has been the threat that the overproduction of doctors, lawyers, and professors (we will ignore clergy) will cause practitioners to sink down into the mass of poorly paid, low-status service workers. The second threat to liberal professionals has been the displacement of these high-status but old-fashioned artisans by innovative organizations that can provide consumers with equal or better services much more cheaply, with some combination of factory-style specialization and technology: Medicine Inc., Law Inc., and Higher Education Inc.

To keep their fees and wages artificially high in an era of mass democracy, the medical, legal, and academic professions around 1900 engaged in a wave of cartelization, forming self-regulating professional associations to forestall direct government regulation in an age of universal suffrage. The bureaucratization of the professions resulted in the migration of elite professional instruction from the offices of practitioners into specialized law schools and business schools. Schools of architecture, public policy, and communications were created even more recently.

With the exception of schools of business and architecture, which still offer undergraduate degrees, most of these professional schools in the last century have further limited entry into professional cartels by requiring a BA as a prerequisite for admission to a graduate program of instruction.

The civil rights revolution and feminism diversified America's White Anglo-Saxon Protestant (WASP)-dominated, male-dominated oligarchy, but the unstated purpose of the modern American university—to perpetuate largely hereditary class distinctions—has remained and even grown in importance. One result of the replacement of apprenticeships for both professions and trades with postcollege professional schools and post–high school technical schools in the last century has been to deepen the social distinction between genteel professions, which require graduate degrees on top of undergraduate degrees, and vulgar working-class trades. The social prestige factor may explain why, among the 48 percent of Americans in 2019 who were engaged in any education, however limited, after high school, 66 percent of undergraduate enrollment was in four-year institutions and only 34 percent in two-year institutions like community colleges.[12] But for the snobbish profession/trade distinction, the ratio might be reversed.

To further minimize the pool of potential economic competitors, the professions imposed generalist-oriented licensing exams requiring knowledge of many subjects, in the case of doctors and lawyers, although not in the case of professors. Meanwhile, professional regulations, mostly written and enforced by the guild organizations of the liberal professions themselves, made it all but impossible for private sector entrepreneurs to modernize the provision and lower the cost of medical, legal, and academic services.

Both of these strategies to save the liberal professions—keeping fees high by limiting entry, and maintaining the work style of the autonomous artisan rather than the factory team worker—have been failing over the last few decades. Law schools and PhD programs, motivated by the desire to keep tuition revenues flowing, have turned out far too many lawyers and PhDs for the few well-paid jobs that are available, creating a proletariat of underemployed, low-wage, often part-time lawyers and academics.

In medicine and law, the old model of the generalist who is self-employed or belongs to a partnership with a handful of others is being replaced by factory-style organization. In Europe, most physicians have long been employed by hospitals. But it is only in the last generation that most American physicians have become salaried employees of hospitals and other health-care organizations, rather than independent practitioners. Meanwhile, large law firms are growing into law factories. From the perspective of the old-time genteel lawyer this is a tragedy, but it is progress from the point of view of the modern consumer, who buys manufactured goods made by factory workers, not by self-employed blacksmiths who keep their own hours.

Tenured university professors are among the last of the old, generalist liberal professionals in the United States. They belong to a dying species. Already, according to some estimates, three-quarters of American undergraduates are taught by non-tenure-track (NTT) faculty (the number is somewhat lower but still high when for-profit colleges are excluded). Most of these NTTs are poorly paid graduate students or PhDs who live from contract to contract, often teaching at several colleges or universities in a single semester while making less money than many plumbers and electricians. Ironically, for an institution whose members are mostly progressive Democrats, the American university resembles a Victorian sweatshop, with a small group of privileged managers and workers lording it over a swelling mass of exploited, underpaid, non-unionized proles.

Given the shift of the teaching load from well-paid tenured professors to low-wage adjuncts and lecturers, you might expect tuition bills to go down for American students. After all, most of their classroom instructors are making next to nothing! Instead, tuitions at American universities for decades have risen faster than the rate of economic growth or inflation, leading many students to take on debt to pay for their educational credential.

Where is all the money going? Faculty compensation has not risen significantly in the last generation, thanks to the cost savings made possible by the exploitation of low-wage adjuncts and lecturers. Some of the money from rising university costs is going to fancy buildings and recreational facilities, but most of it fuels administrative bloat—overpaid university presidents and other top officials, whose excessive salaries are partly justified by their need to supervise an expanding caste of university bureaucrats with make-work jobs like DEI (diversity, equity, and inclusion) deans and administrators, hired as a concession to left-wing identity politics activists. In 2018, Mark Perry, a professor of economics at the University of Michigan, calculated that the university at which he taught had nearly a hundred "diversity administrators," of whom more than twenty-five made more than $100,000 a year.[13]

In a productive economic sector, laborsaving technology and/or the factory-style division of labor result in what might be called the virtuous circle of industrialism: prices for consumers fall, wages for workers rise, and the ratio of managers to productive workers stays the same or shrinks. In the American university, however, technological stagnation, artisanal production, and administrative bloat result in rising prices for consumers, falling wages for the majority of productive workers (nontenured instructors), and more unproductive managers.

Apart from useful research, most of which could be done just as well in independent institutes, the product of all but the most prestigious American universities consists of diplomas that are rendered progressively more worthless each year thanks to credential inflation. According to the Federal Reserve of New York, the underemployment rate for recent college grads—that is, the percentage working in jobs that do not require a college degree—was 40 percent at the end of March 2021. True, workers with college diplomas tend to make more than those without them, but at least some of the college premium may be the result of underemployed college graduates pushing high school graduates into even worse jobs.

The surplus pool of college graduates has allowed many American businesses to use diplomas as tools to screen applicants for jobs that in the past did not require college degrees. Deprived of the ability to test the aptitude of applicants by the Supreme Court's decision in *Griggs v. Duke Power Co.* (1971), which disallowed tests in which there are racial disparities in test results, many employers may be using college degrees as a substitute.[14] A four-year bachelor's degree may not be necessary for a job that a high school graduate can perform, but the diploma is evidence that the applicant is disciplined and can complete assigned tasks.

The credential arms race, then, is the direct result of the decline in worker bargaining power in general and the annihilation of private sector organized labor in the United States in particular. In the process of breaking the power of labor unions, American business eliminated many middle-income jobs that did not require a college degree, resulting in a desperate scramble by many

Americans to obtain a middle-class lifestyle by investing time and money in acquiring the tickets for participation in licensed cartels or cartel-like professions. How the credential arms race harms American society in one area after another, from partisan politics and identity politics to family formation, will be explored in the next chapter.

CHAPTER EIGHT

Cascade Effect

How Bad Jobs and the Credential Arms Race Make Every Social Crisis Worse

Every major social crisis Americans face today—falling fertility, the loneliness epidemic, bitter conflicts over racial and gender identity, and growing partisan polarization in politics—is worsened if not caused by the collapse of worker power.

Here is how the cascade effect works. Low wages, along with the expensive credential arms race, lead many Americans to delay, and sometimes forgo, marriage, family formation, and childbearing, leading to fertility rates far below the levels needed for maintenance of the U.S. population at its present level without high and economically harmful rates of unskilled immigration. Low wages and insecure jobs also contribute to many of the pathologies of the working poor, including disconnection from the workforce, lack of friends and social life, drug addiction, and "deaths of despair." Identity politics, which would exist anyway in a diverse society of different races, ethnic groups, and religions, is worsened by its weaponization in the struggles of too many college-educated Americans competing for too few well-paying positions. Last but not least, the collapse of private sector organized labor as a major political force has produced an overall decline in the political influence of working-class Americans of all races and regions, replacing the transactional politics of the New Deal era with bitter ideological struggles among factions of the college-educated, affluent overclass.

For centuries children in the English-speaking countries have learned a proverb that has equivalents in other European languages ("want of" in this context means "lack of"):

> *For want of a nail, the shoe was lost.*
> *For want of a shoe, the horse was lost.*
> *For want of a horse, the rider was lost.*
> *For want of a rider, the battle was lost.*
> *For want of a battle, the kingdom was lost.*
> *And all for the want of a horseshoe nail.*

Thanks to a similar cascade effect, for want of good wages, American society is in danger.

Let's begin with the demographic crisis. The marital and reproductive behavior of various classes in different civilized societies has always been influenced by the requirements of social status and property ownership.

In the twenty-first-century United States, as in most other advanced industrial nations, most people are wage or salary earners. The most important form of property is not a farm or a business or a house but a credential that gives the wage earner access to a stream of income—in most cases a stream of income from an employer, but in some cases income directly from customers or clients paying for licensed professional or technical services.

Whether in the form of college degrees or occupational licenses, credentials are usually time-consuming as well as expensive to obtain. As we saw in the last chapter, access to the best jobs in the United States increasingly requires not merely a four-year college degree but also a graduate or professional degree of some kind, like an MA, an MBA, a law degree, or a PhD. The master's degree is the new BA. Thanks to credential inflation, the PhD may soon be the new high school diploma.

The greater the number of degrees that people obtain, the more years they must spend in higher education. This explains why American workers with graduate and professional degrees tend to marry and form families later than those whose educations end with high school or a bachelor's degree.[1]

In return for postponing marriage and family life, successful professionals and managers with advanced degrees win the competition for access to cartelized professions like those of doctors and lawyers or full-time employment by medium to large firms that informally collaborate with their peers in illegal but tolerated wage-fixing "salary band" schemes. Those who do not go to college, or attend college but drop out at some point, usually must settle for inferior jobs and can never achieve the economic stability and middle-class lifestyle of which they dream.

Credentialism contributes to the "diploma divide" in marriage in the twenty-first-century United States. The most educated Americans are most likely to be married and most likely to stay married. Less educated Americans are more likely to never be married or, if they are married, to be divorced. Both working-class and college-educated Americans tend to live with their partners before marriage, but cohabitation among working-class couples is less likely to lead to formal marriage and more likely to break down in its absence.[2]

To be sure, calling this the "diploma divide" is misleading. The main factor is the difference between good and bad jobs, not between degrees, which are mere tickets to good jobs. The marital diploma divide is about money, not about scholarship. Financial stress is a major cause of disruption in relationships and divorce. College-educated couples are more likely to stay together because they are more financially secure than working-class couples.

At the same time that there is a growing class and credential divide in marriage, birthrates are dropping below the numbers needed to replace the U.S. population. Advocates of the theory of "the second demographic transition" sometimes attribute the collapse in total fertility rate to the voluntary choice of parents to limit the number of children they have. The evidence suggests otherwise. The chief reason for falling birthrates in the United States is delayed marriage and non-marriage, not a preference for fewer children. While few contemporary couples want the large families of premodern agrarian societies, polls consistently show that most American parents wish they had more children than they end up having. The American fertility rate of 1.77 is far below the average number of children that American women, native and immigrant alike, desire: 2.7. When asked why, parents who wish they had more children often blame inadequate incomes or the need to postpone marriage and childbearing until a level of economic security or professional rank has been achieved.[3]

Delayed marriage is the main reason that couples do not have as many children as they want, given the biological limits to female fertility. And the main reason for delayed marriage and postponed childbirth is credentialism—the need to amass one or more university diplomas, in order to have access to a good-paying, stable job as a precondition for marriage and family formation.

In most industrial countries, birthrates have fallen below the number needed to replace the population. This has occurred both in countries with generous welfare states and high levels of unionization and in those without; social democratic Finland has experienced one of the steepest declines. The key factors in otherwise different countries appear to be delays in childbearing by women seeking educational credentials and the difficulties caused for child care by participation of mothers in the workforce. A 2019 study of women in the U.K., for example, found that "increasing attendance in higher education has a largely direct effect on early childbearing up to 25 years, resulting in a substantial increase in childlessness."[4] More diplomas for fewer children may be a bad trade-off for many, given the reality of degree inflation, which results in increasing time and money wasted on higher education to obtain credentials that are not really necessary for many jobs.

Credentialism causes far fewer Americans to be born than might have been in an alternate world in which obtaining stable, well-paid jobs did not so often require people to spend their twenties and sometimes their thirties in school. As one older woman of my acquaintance complained, "I wanted grandchildren and all I get are diplomas."

Credential inflation plays a part in what might be called the American social crisis as well. For those who fail to climb the credential ladder out of the pulverized and powerless American working class, the American dream can turn into the American nightmare.

In the 2010s the economists Anne Case and Angus Deaton shocked the world by documenting an epidemic of "deaths of despair" caused by suicide, alcohol, opioid addiction, and other factors among working-class white Americans. Deaths of despair were concentrated in deindustrialized regions of the Midwest and South from which good-paying union jobs in factories had disappeared as a result of Chinese import competition and offshoring by U.S. companies to low-wage workforces in China, Mexico, and other countries.[5]

More than a loss of income is involved. For men and women in midlife to go from stable, decently paying jobs to insecure work or dependence on welfare is humiliating. At the same time, the young are demoralized by growing up in communities with boarded-up factories and stores and shrinking populations, where more money sometimes is to be made in petty or organized crime or reliance on public assistance than in regular jobs.

Many of these same social pathologies earlier afflicted urban African Americans and others when factories had abandoned northeastern and midwestern urban areas, sending entire neighborhoods and metro areas into decline.[6] The crack epidemic in blighted urban America in the late twentieth century foreshadowed the opioid epidemic that swept rural and small-town America in the twenty-first. The patronizing phrase "left behind" implied that there were plenty of good jobs waiting, if only the victims of sectoral or regional economic change would move or upgrade their educational credentials. But as we have seen in earlier chapters, great numbers of good jobs with good wages and benefits to replace the unionized manufacturing and manufacturing-related jobs that have been eliminated by offshoring and de-unionization are not being created in the United States.

Another intangible cost that contributes to the social crisis of the downwardly mobile American working class of all races is what the French social theorist Émile Durkheim called "anomie"—normlessness or disorientation or alienation. Here again the destruction of private trade unions by American businesses and their allies in government has had ripple effects throughout society. Many unions had been the center of the social lives of their members. The collapse of unions, along with the decline of church attendance, is creating greater disconnection and isolation among members of the American working class of all races than existed a few generations ago.

Civic associations have failed to fill the gap. The local mass-membership organizations that flourished in the middle of the twentieth century, like the Shriners and Jaycees, have been displaced by a new kind of nonprofit organization, funded by the rich or by small donations and employing a college-educated over-class staff.[7] The professional staff of these "astroturf" organizations tend to view local working-class populations rather as nineteenth-century European and American missionaries viewed non-Western "natives"—as primitives in need of rescue from barbarism by enlightened saviors, not as neighbors and peers whose major problem is a lack of economic and political power.

The greater rates of non-marriage and divorce among working-class Americans also contribute to anomie. Parents often meet neighbors and colleagues through the shared activities of their children. The link to a wider community that the family provides is not available to men and women who are un-marriageable because of their low wages and inadequate credentials, and may not be available either to married partners or members of a co-habiting couple after a breakup. What was once the rich associational life of much of the American working class, centered on unions, churches, clubs, and local political parties and supplemented by friendship with neighbors, in all too many places has become a social desert.[8]

Between 1990 and 2021, the number of American women who reported that they had six or more close friends fell from 41 percent to 24 percent, with 10 percent saying they had no close friends at all. The decline of friendship among American men has been even more pronounced, falling from 55 percent with at least six close friends in 1990 to 27 percent, while the number of men reporting no close friends has risen in the last thirty years from 3 percent to 15 percent.[9] Friendship, like family formation, is withering away in the United States.

To the demographic crisis and the social crisis, we can add the American identity crisis. While the social crisis tends to affect working-class Americans who never took part in, or dropped out of, the credential arms race, the identity crisis is driven by college-educated Americans who fear that not enough good jobs are available for those with their qualifications.

What has been called "the Great Awokening" of the 2010s and 2020s has many of the features of the Protestant revivals of the

American past. Instead of confessing their sins, woke Americans confess their racism, sexism, and homophobia, using a curiously stilted, liturgical language. Baptism into the new faith of woke progressivism brings with it a new vocabulary—"birthing people" for "mothers"—and a catechism: "some men can get pregnant," and "color blindness is a form of racism." As with religious conversions, the born-again woke may adopt new identities, sometimes racial or ethnic but more frequently related to gender, like "nonbinary."

Paradoxically, although denouncing white America is one of the rituals of performative woke leftism, the woke left is much whiter than the U.S. population in general. Studies have shown that affluent, college-educated whites are more likely to adopt woke attitudes and language than working-class black and Hispanic Americans, who tend to be moderate cultural conservatives.[10]

Using a phrase coined by the author Peter Turchin, many have attributed wokeness to "the overproduction of elites"—in particular, to the overproduction of college graduates. Turchin's cyclic theory of history can be disputed, but given the social base of the Great Awokening among white college graduates, the concept is plausible when more narrowly applied.[11]

Thanks to the credential arms race, far more young Americans apply to colleges and universities today than in earlier generations. Increasingly, college applicants are distinguishing themselves from the competition in application letters by means of their "identity credentials," emphasizing their membership in this or that racial or sexual minority or weaving into the letter phrases from the ritualized "social justice" lexicon that might appeal to the overwhelmingly progressive university admissions committees. One applicant got into Stanford in 2017 by writing an application letter that consisted of nothing more than one hundred repetitions of the slogan "#BlackLivesMatter."[12]

The competition among graduates is just as fierce as among applicants. According to the Federal Reserve in 2020, 41 percent of recent college graduates work in occupations that do not require a college diploma.[13] A 2021 study by Burning Glass found that two-thirds of the four-in-ten college graduates who are underemployed in their first job will still be underemployed five years later, and of those, three-quarters will be working in non-college jobs after a decade.[14]

One strategy adopted by elite institutions to absorb surplus graduates, particularly those with degrees of limited market value in gender studies or minority studies, has been to multiply the number of well-paid make-work jobs related to "diversity, equity, and inclusion"—college campus DEI bureaucracies, corporate HR offices, consultancies that specialize in "diversity training" for firms and government agencies and nonprofits. Illegal but government-tolerated quota systems ensure that many of these make-work jobs will go to workers whose race, sex, or gender self-identification gives them an edge over their white or male or heterosexual competitors.

In other career tracks in highly prestigious professions and companies, ideology rather than identity can be deployed for self-advancement. Office Machiavels can weaponize "wokeness" to bring down supervisors or other colleagues standing in the way of their career ambitions, by "calling them out" for "microaggressions" and pressuring risk-averse management to fire those who are denounced, thereby opening up new organizational career pathways for the denouncers.

The ever-changing woke lexicon serves the function of a code that allows elite insiders to discriminate against outsiders, whose lack of knowledge of what is politically correct this week can be as damning as a southern accent in a Wall Street law firm or a cockney accent in a London barrister's office. For a decade or two, the test of membership in the college-educated American overclass was knowing that you should say "people of color" instead of "colored people." In the last few years, however, the new shibboleth is "BIPOC" (Black, Indigenous, and People of Color), so that saying "people of color" now not only is a faux pas but may be a bad career move in many elite American institutions. As this book goes to press, a new shibboleth is being popularized within the American overclass to distinguish elite insiders from outsiders, "ALAANA" (African, Latinx, Asian, Arab, Native American).

In short, one unanticipated but major social result of the credential arms race has been a spin-off competition: the *identity credential arms race*.

Like other pathologies of contemporary American society, today's partisan polarization is influenced indirectly by the decline of worker power.

Mid-twentieth-century America not only had the first (and last) mass middle class in American history but also was built on mass politics. The political system was shaped by the influence of mass-membership organizations: trade unions, the once-powerful farmers' organizations, well-attended churches, and fraternal and civic organizations. The Democratic and Republican parties themselves were national federations of state and local parties, in which great numbers of Americans took part in some way.

The result was what the journalist John Chamberlain in his book *The American Stakes* (1940) described as "the broker state."[15] Politicians and government administrators brokering deals among the organized groups of organized blocs naturally tended to produce a transactional politics with plenty of room for compromise among the big players—business, labor, the farm lobby, urban political machines.[16]

That world has vanished. The destruction of private sector unions by American business and government has eliminated the major institution that empowered working people, apart from their participation as voters in the political system. Half a century ago, labor leaders like Walter Reuther and George Meany were household names, powerful leaders who negotiated with presidents and congressional leaders as well as corporate executives. Today many union members themselves would be hard-pressed to name any national union officials. Public sector unions continue to influence the Democratic Party, but the decline of private sector unions has resulted in the near monopoly of lobbying about private sector economic issues by business interests, influencing Democrats and Republicans alike.

Meanwhile, the parties themselves have changed from mass-membership federations into mere brands bankrolled by billionaires and corporations and responsive chiefly to members of the college-educated overclass. The decision of both national parties in the 1970s to select candidates in open-party primary elections or caucuses, rather than in conventions dominated by career politicians, was intended to make American politics more democratic. Instead, the primary system has made American politics more oligarchic.

For decades primary voters as a share of eligible voters has fluctuated between 10 and 30 percent, compared with around 40 percent in midterm general elections and around 60 percent turnout in general elections in presidential election years.[17] Moreover, the small number of voters who take part in party primaries are not typical of their own parties. They are better educated, more affluent, and more ideological than most Democrats and Republicans. A study in 2018 found that 62 percent of Democratic primary voters and 58 percent of Republican primary voters had bachelor's degrees or more, compared with only about a third of the American public. At a time when the average household income was $60,309, more than half of the primary voters in each party came from households making more than $75,000 a year.[18]

Affluent Democrats and affluent Republicans alike tend to be motivated by "post-material values" and passionate about polarizing social issues like abortion or gun control, unlike America's multiracial working-class majority, whose chief concerns according to pollsters are quotidian issues like the economy, health care, and safety from crime. The well-educated and well-off Democrats who are overrepresented in Democratic primaries drag the party to the left of most Democrats on social issues. At the same time, the Republican Party is dragged to the right of median Republican voters on social issues, not by the ignorant working-class yahoos demonized by snobbish progressives, but by petit bourgeois and professional-class Republicans motivated by culture war zeal.

Along with upscale, educated, hyper-ideological primary voters, the selectorate of each party includes affluent party donors. As Martin Gilens and Benjamin I. Page showed in a celebrated study in 2014, elected officials of both parties tend to side with the donors against the voters in the party, on issues where the two groups have opposing views.[19] As a whole, the American donor class forms a relatively homogeneous bipartisan establishment whose members have more in common with each other than with most Democrats or Republicans. The oligarchs of the American campaign donor class tend to be more liberal than the general public on social issues, as well as more free market oriented and more in favor of free trade, mass immigration, and American military interventions abroad. Members of the American donor class, from the elites of Silicon Valley and Hollywood who support Democrats to the fossil fuel and agribusiness executives who are more likely to fund Republicans, along with Wall Street donors who can be found on both sides, tend to share a hostility to organized labor in their own private sector industries.

All of this explains the otherwise puzzling gap between the policy preferences of Democratic and Republican voters and the actions of their elected representatives. Elected officials in both national parties respond chiefly to their elite selectorates—affluent primary or caucus voters and donors—not to the party electorates made up of ordinary, mostly working-class voters of diverse backgrounds.

Forty-seven percent of Republican voters approve of labor unions, but almost all Republican elected officials are hostile to organized labor, thanks to the party's overwhelmingly libertarian and corporate donors and its well-off primary voters.[20] Majorities of black, Hispanic, and Asian Americans, who vote disproportionately for Democrats, have long wanted police funding to stay the same or increase.[21] But many affluent white progressives and elite nonwhite activists have led many cities under Democratic rule to slash funding for the police, tolerate high levels of property theft, and eliminate bail requirements, during a historic crime wave.

Majorities of African Americans (62 percent), Hispanic Americans (65 percent), and Asian Americans (58 percent), who vote disproportionately for Democrats, as well as non-Hispanic white Americans (78 percent), who are mostly Republican, agree that "colleges should not consider race in admissions," according to the Pew Research Center in 2019.[22] Meanwhile, major universities in the United States, in which elite Democrats make up almost all of the professors and administrators, in the name of "diversity, equity, and inclusion," have adopted de facto race-based quota systems for admissions and faculty hires and even classroom curricula. The pressure for rigid race and gender quotas in all areas of American society is not coming from below.

Even the street-fighting zealots of the far left, like antifa, and the far right, like the rioters who stormed the U.S. Capitol on January 6, are disproportionately members of the American elite, not the working class. Investing in "black bloc" anarchist outfits is expensive, and so is traveling from city to city to take part in leftist protests and sometimes to engage in violent clashes or vandalism.[23] Likewise, the militant supporters of President Trump who could afford plane tickets and hotel rooms in Washington, D.C., as the price of taking part in the pro-Trump "Stop the Steal" protest on January 6 and the subsequent riot and ransacking of the U.S. Capitol were not poor.

As the influence of the organized working class diminishes, and as politics becomes a game for college-credentialed professional elites and the wealthy, representative democracy becomes an arena for the rule-or-ruin feuds of ambitious oligarchs and their retainers.

All four crises—the demographic crisis, the social crisis, the identity crisis, and the political crisis of partisan polarization—might exist in some form without the collapse of American worker power and the resulting low wages and credential arms race. But there is little doubt that higher wages at the bottom, and a restoration of both individual and collective worker bargaining power, would reduce many of the tensions in American society. In the concluding chapters, I will suggest how worker power might be restored, as part of a national strategy to boost long-term national growth while sharing its gains among all Americans.

CHAPTER NINE

The Myths of Neoliberal Globalization

We're number two—and falling! That should be America's slogan when it comes to national shares of global markets in manufacturing. The United States has been eclipsed by China as the world's dominant manufacturing power and has lost one industry and critical supply chain after another, mostly to China and other contemporary East Asian economic nationalist states—not just low-tech, labor-intensive industries like textiles, but also high-tech, capital-intensive, advanced manufacturing industries like commercial shipbuilding, which is dominated by China, South Korea, and Japan.[1]

A single Chinese company, DJI, produces more than half of all civilian drones that are purchased worldwide.[2] Meanwhile, in the last three decades, the United States has lost 70 percent of its semiconductor manufacturing industry to other countries, in particular Taiwan. The global market share of American machine tool manufacturing, another key industry, has plunged from 28 percent in 1965 to 5 percent today. America's share of civilian jet engine exports fell from 70 percent to 39 percent between 1991 and 2009, while its share of global solar cell manufacturing declined by three-quarters in a mere six years from 2006 to 2013.[3] Chinese companies make 60 percent of the world's wind turbines.[4] The only American company among the top fifteen wind turbine manufacturers, GE Renewable Energy, contributed a mere 10 percent to the global market in 2018.[5] In 2020, China made 76 percent of the world's lithium-ion batteries, essential for electric cars. The United States made only 8 percent.[6]

The COVID-19 crisis that began in 2020 dramatically revealed the dependence of the United States on other countries for basic drugs and personal protective equipment. In 2018, Chinese pharmaceutical firms dominated the U.S. markets for antibiotics (97 percent), ibuprofen (90 percent), hydrocortisone (91 percent), vitamin C (90 percent), acetaminophen (70 percent), and heparin (40–45 percent). Thanks to outsourcing to take advantage of low wages compared with those in the United States, 80 percent of active pharmaceutical ingredients used in American drugs are thought to come from China and India. Forty percent of generic and over-the-counter drugs in the United States come from India.[7] And despite the economic malaise that followed the crash of Japan's economic bubble in the 1990s, in 2020 Japan manufactured 47 percent of the world's robots.[8]

America's share of global markets would have declined to some degree as Asia and other regions industrialized. But the rapid dismantling of America's productive economy in the last few decades is primarily the result of the hunger of American corporations for cheap labor in other countries.

Why would any government tolerate this destructive behavior on the part of its own companies and their investors? Why would a nation like the United States at the height of its industrial power allow its own corporations to rip up the national industrial base by offshoring production in one major industry after another?

Part of the answer is simple corruption: corporate influence on policy makers by campaign donations and other methods, including jobs as lobbyists or corporate board members for former public servants and legal bribes and rewards, like the huge sums from corporations and financial firms for mediocre speeches of the kind that have gone to Ronald Reagan and Bill and Hillary Clinton and Barack Obama after their terms in office. Another part of the answer might be called "the curse of hegemony"—the willingness of the United States to cede entire industries to foreign allies and protectorates, as long as they deferred to American global military primacy. And a third factor was the complacent belief that a permanent American lead in technological innovation would somehow compensate for the permanent loss of the ability to manufacture the products of innovation.

In the last generation, the American public was not told by officials and opinion leaders that globalization was primarily driven by corporations seeking to save money on labor costs and avoid unions by shutting down American factories and firing American workers and moving production to low-wage workers abroad. Nor were Americans told that neoliberal globalization was a deliberate public policy choice, with harm to some and benefits for others, and that there were alternatives, with different patterns of harm and benefit.

Instead, the public was falsely told by many politicians, pundits, and professors that few or no domestic workers were harmed by either offshoring or mass low-wage immigration, that everyone or almost everyone in the United States and similar industrial democracies benefited from these policies, and that anyone who questioned this happy-talk narrative was motivated by xenophobic bigotry or ignorant of elementary economics.

Between the 1980s and the 2020s, ideas about open borders policies in trade and immigration that had formerly been dismissed as crackpot doctrines of the libertarian fringe became the respectable orthodoxy from the center-left to the center-right. The *New York Times* columnist Thomas Friedman declared, "I wrote a column supporting the Cafta, the Caribbean Free Trade initiative. I didn't even know what was in it. I just knew two words: free trade."[9] Robert Bartley, the longtime editor of *The Wall Street Journal*, repeatedly proposed a constitutional amendment limited to five words: "There shall be open borders."[10] One of the most strident and apocalyptic advocates of neoliberal globalization was Martin Wolf, a columnist for the *Financial Times*, a publication whose name tells you everything you need to know about its audience: "Liberals, social democrats, and moderate conservatives are on the same side in the great battles against religious fanatics, obscurantists, extreme environmentalists, fascists, Marxists, and, of course, contemporary anti-globalisers."[11]

In "Wrong All Along," American Compass, a think tank critical of neoliberal orthodoxy, has compiled amusing samples of the hyperbole used by promoters of NAFTA, the WTO, and permanent trade relations with China in the 1990s and first decade of the twenty-first century.[12] There was the "Can't Stop, Won't Stop" fallacy. The British prime minister Tony Blair declared that "globalization is a force of nature, not a policy; it is a fact."[13] President Bill Clinton agreed with his neoliberal British ally: "Yet globalization is not something we can hold off or turn off. It is the economic equivalent of a force of nature—like wind or water.... But there is no point in denying the existence of wind or water, or trying to make them go away." In addition, American Compass identifies the "End of History" fallacy (free trade will bring democracy and freedom to China) and "Disparaging Disagreement: No One Disagrees, So Please Ignore Those Who Disagree."

Then there was the "Better Jobs" fallacy, endorsed by the economist Larry Summers, Clinton's secretary of the Treasury, who declared that "the economic and commercial benefits of granting PNTR [Permanent Normal Trading Relations to China] are significant *and all on the side of US businesses and workers* [emphasis added]."[14] Poor China was outwitted by wily Americans and got the raw end of the deal, according to Summers.

The oft-repeated claim in the corporate and financial media that no significant economists question the benefits of free trade for all sides has always been false. Some of the strongest criticism of free trade dogma has come from highly respected thinkers within the mainstream economics academy. In his 1933 essay "National Self-Sufficiency," John Maynard Keynes wrote, "We do not wish, therefore, to be at the mercy of world forces working out, or trying to work out, some uniform equilibrium according to the ideal principles, if they can be called such, of laissez-faire capitalism." In a world of diverse and sometimes incompatible social systems Keynes argued "that we all need to be as free as possible of interference from economic changes elsewhere, in order to make our own favourite experiments towards the ideal social republic of the future; and that a deliberate movement towards greater national self-sufficiency and economic isolation will make our task easier, in so far as it can be accomplished without excessive economic cost."[15]

In the second half of the twentieth century the British economist Nicholas Kaldor demonstrated that the argument for free trade from comparative advantage falls apart, when one trading partner has industries that enjoy increasing returns to scale, like most manufacturing industries.[16] Another blow to free trade orthodoxy came in 2001, when William J. Baumol, one of America's leading economists, and Ralph Gomory, a leading mathematician, showed in *Global Trade and Conflicting National Interests* that some countries could benefit at the expense of others in a world economy based on technological innovation and giant firms.[17]

The best known of the heretical dissenters from free trade orthodoxy was Paul A. Samuelson, the dean of American academic economists—and the uncle of Larry Summers. In a 2004 article in *The Journal of Economic Perspectives*, Samuelson upset orthodox free traders by demonstrating that the combination of free trade and mass migration could harm a country. Samuelson concluded with a highly equivocal statement about policy: "It does not follow from my corrections and emendations that nations should or should not introduce selective protectionisms" in the areas of trade and immigration.[18]

Notwithstanding these eminent examples, the power of conformity and groupthink among American academic economists ensured that those within their ranks who question simple-minded models of free trade risked being ostracized. The career of Paul Krugman provides an illustration.

In 1987, still a promising young economist, Krugman published a paper in *The Journal of Economic Perspectives* with the daring title "Is Free Trade Passé?" in which he observed,

> If there were an Economist's Creed, it would surely contain the affirmations "I understand the Principle of Comparative Advantage" and "I advocate Free Trade." ... Yet the case for free trade is currently more in doubt than at any time since the 1817 publication of Ricardo's *Principles of Political Economy* ...

because of the changes that have recently taken place in the
theory of international trade itself.... There is still a case for
free trade as a good policy, and as a useful target in the prac-
tical world of politics, but it can never again be asserted as the
policy that economic theory tells us is always right.[19]

Only a few years later, however, Krugman became one of the
most vehement critics of scholars, public servants, and journalists
who questioned the offshoring of American manufacturing or imports from mercantilist nations or low-wage countries, doing his
best to destroy their reputations in the eyes of the transatlantic
media and business and academic establishments. Among the many
whom Krugman denounced in the 1990s as heretics who devi-
ated from free-market orthodoxy were Bill Clinton, Robert Reich,
Laura D'Andrea Tyson, Larry Summers, Jeffrey Garten, Robert
Kuttner, James Fallows, and yours truly.[20]

With the zeal of a repentant heretic, in a 1993 speech to the
American Economic Association, Krugman suggested that his own
unorthodox theories about trade should not be taught in undergraduate economics courses, so that students would not be exposed
to doubts about free trade.[21] Ironically, when the Royal Swedish
Academy of Sciences awarded the Sveriges Riksbank Prize in
Economic Sciences in Memory of Alfred Nobel (the so-called
Nobel Prize in Economics) to Krugman in 2008, they claimed it
was in part for his early work in strategic trade theory—work that
he himself had disavowed. To be sure, many observers thought
the Swedes were simply rewarding Krugman, a Democrat, for reg-

ularly denouncing the Republican president George W. Bush in his *New York Times* column. The following year the newly elected Barack Obama, who had yet to do anything as president, was awarded the Nobel Peace Prize for not being George W. Bush.

Donald Trump shocked the globalist establishment on both sides of the Atlantic with his unapologetic American economic nationalism. But even while repudiating Trump's unilateralism, his successor as president, Joe Biden, has built on some of Trump's efforts to reshore manufacturing and critical material mining and refining in the United States while adding new initiatives. America's deepening trade war and cold war with authoritarian, mercantilist China, and the rupture in trade between Russia and the United States and its European allies following Russia's invasion of Ukraine, have brought an end to the dream of a rule-governed global market under unchallenged U.S. military hegemony. "Industrial policy," once a taboo phrase among elite Democrats and Republicans alike, is now considered a legitimate kind of public policy again.

Tony Blair was wrong when he said that "globalization is a force of nature, not a policy; it is a fact." And Bill Clinton was wrong when he declared that globalization "is the economic equivalent of a force of nature—like wind or water." Globalization was and is a deliberate government policy, undertaken by the government of the United States and other national governments to serve the interests of politically powerful employers and investors who seek to use global labor arbitrage, in the form of offshoring or immigration, in order to cripple or destroy organized labor and weaken the bargaining power of workers at home and abroad.

When all of the specious arguments for wage-driven offshoring have failed, defenders of pro-employer, anti-worker globalization policies sometimes assert that it is too late to undo them now. On October 10, 2019, in a *Bloomberg* essay titled "What Economists (Including Me) Got Wrong About Globalization," Paul Krugman admitted that "we are in effect importing the services of less educated workers, putting downward pressure on the demand for such workers in the U.S." But according to Krugman, the only correct cure for the harm done by indiscriminate free trade is more indiscriminate free trade: "So while the 1990s consensus on the effect of globalization hasn't stood the test of time, its shortcomings don't make a case for protectionism now. We might have done things differently if we had known what was coming, but that's not a good reason to turn back the clock."[22]

Like Krugman, Stephen Roach, formerly of Morgan Stanley Asia, claims that it is too late to rebuild U.S. manufacturing now: "It has taken more than twenty years for China, a broad network of associated suppliers, and U.S. multinationals to assemble this complex global sourcing platform [based in China]. If Humpty Dumpty is pushed off the wall, it will take considerable time to put all the pieces back together again."[23]

The short-term economic costs of partly reversing neoliberal globalization, by means of a combination of strategic trade policies that reshore key industrial supply chains with selective immigration policies, might be significant. But those costs are outweighed by the costs to American prosperity, American national industrial dynamism, and American national security of continuing to permit corporations to deindustrialize the United States while swelling America's low-wage, welfare-dependent workforce so that corporate managers and shareholders can enjoy higher profits by paying less to workers here and abroad.

Rejecting the myths of neoliberal globalization frees us to consider an alternate policy of strategic trade and immigration in the national interest that can rebuild American productive capacity and American worker power at the same time.

CHAPTER TEN

Beyond Global Arbitrage

Trade, Immigration, and
the Next American System

In 1832, a twenty-three-year-old candidate for the Illinois state legislature who belonged to the Whig Party began his campaign by endorsing the party platform:

> *Fellow-citizens*: I presume you all know who I am. I am humble Abraham Lincoln. I have been solicited by many friends to become a candidate for the Legislature. My politics are short and sweet, like the old woman's dance. I am in favor of a national bank. I am in favor of the internal improvement system, and a high protective tariff. These are my sentiments and political principles. If elected, I shall be thankful; if not it will be all the same.[1]

Lincoln was describing the "American System," a program for the economic development of the United States by means of tariff-based import substitution industrialization, infrastructure, and national finance. Lincoln's hero and role model, the Kentucky senator Henry Clay, had formulated the American System, building on the policies advocated by Alexander Hamilton, the first U.S. secretary of the Treasury in the administration of George Washington.

Between the Civil War and the New Deal, Lincoln's Republican Party, the Hamiltonian heir to the prewar Whigs, presided over the government-sponsored industrialization of the United States, achieving most of the goals of the American System—national banking laws (rather than a single national bank, although the Federal Reserve came to serve as one in some ways), internal improvements (railroads paid for in many cases by federal land grants to railroad companies), and high protective tariffs that sheltered American infant industries from British and European import competition.

Rather than breaking with the Hamiltonian developmental statism of the Lincoln Republicans, the Roosevelt Democrats of the mid-twentieth-century New Deal era built upon it, even as they paid lip service to the Democratic Party's heroes, Thomas Jefferson and Andrew Jackson. Under FDR and his successors, including the Republicans Eisenhower and Nixon, who ratified much of the New Deal, the federal government promoted and diffused the technologies of the second Industrial Revolution, based on the internal combustion engine and electricity, by means of programs including federal subsidies for highway construction and rural electrification.

As assistant secretary of the U.S. Navy under President Woodrow Wilson, Franklin Delano Roosevelt at Wilson's direction allocated navy funds to subsidize the creation of a national "wireless" monopoly, the Radio Corporation of America, or RCA, which spun off the three major networks—ABC, NBC, and CBS—and played a major role in the development of television and other devices. During the New Deal era from the 1930s to the 1980s, the federal government used airmail to subsidize the development of a domestic U.S. airline industry and created the National Aeronautics and Space Administration to develop rockets and satellites and send astronauts to the moon. Under President Dwight Eisenhower, considerations of national defense in the atomic age as well as economic growth led Congress to fund the interstate highway system. Federal state capitalism in the service of American national industrial policy during the cold war also took the form of Defense Department spending that subsidized much of the development of satellite technology, the computer industry, and the global positioning system, or GPS. The internet began as ARPANET, a Pentagon-funded project to link researchers who had Defense Department contracts.[2]

Neoliberal globalization after the cold war marked a radical break with the successful American developmentalist tradition from the 1790s to the 1980s. Instead of exporting factory products, a neoliberal country exports factories. Instead of using private corporations to promote the national interest, a neoliberal country allows corporations to use the government to promote private corporate interests. The objective of corporations in neoliberal states is not to maximize the foreign consumer markets for goods and services produced by workers in the home economy. Rather, it is to add the largest possible foreign labor pool to the domestic workforce so that the corporations can move production to low-wage workers abroad while selling goods to the home market and other countries.

To put it another way, a developmental state serves the interests of national workers and national manufacturers, to the detriment of multinational corporations and global investors, if necessary. A neoliberal state serves the interests of multinational corporations and global investors, to the detriment of national workers and national manufacturers, if necessary. The alleged well-being of consumers is invoked by the multinationals and their investors as an insincere excuse for global labor arbitrage strategies whose real purpose is to increase short-term corporate profits.

In the aftermath of the failed half-century policy of corporate-driven cheap-labor globalization, the United States should return to the tradition that the economist Robert D. Atkinson and I have described as "national developmentalism." What is needed is a new American System, in the tradition of Hamilton, Clay, Lincoln, FDR, and Eisenhower, and suited to the challenges and opportunities of the information age.[3]

A new American System for the mid-twenty-first century should focus on productivity growth, not workforce growth, as the primary method for increasing gross domestic product.

GDP is a flawed but useful measure of an economy's output, which results from both hours worked and output per worker per hour (per capita productivity). The easiest way to increase GDP without increasing per-worker productivity is simply to increase work hours. This can be done by methods like making existing workers work longer hours, with fewer vacations; by delaying the retirement age; and by increasing the share of working-age adults who are in the workforce—for example, by encouraging or pressuring the mothers of young children to work. Needless to say, increasing GDP by these methods imposes hardships on workers.

Another method of increasing GDP by increasing hours worked, without increasing productivity per worker, is to increase the number of people in the workforce. In the absence of an unlikely baby boom, the workforce can be expanded rapidly by importing immigrants. But if the immigrants are less productive than native and naturalized workers, and are paid less on average, then a massive, immigration-fed increase in population can lower average wages and lower per-worker productivity, even as nominal GDP increases. The economy grows, but the nation gets poorer.

American policy makers should reject strategies to grow GDP

that depend on making workers work longer hours or retire later or by pushing family caregivers into the workforce. They should also reject making the U.S. economy bigger but poorer and less productive by importing the foreign poor in numbers so large that they drive down average wages and productivity. Instead, the focus of national economic policy should be on productivity growth.

Since the Industrial Revolution began, productivity growth has been driven almost entirely by the adoption of laborsaving technology. Laborsaving technology can either replace human labor entirely, as a washing machine replaces a human washing clothes, or complement labor, as an assembly-line robot can allow one human assembly-line worker to do what could earlier be done only by three assembly-line workers.

Whether complementary technology leads to job loss depends in part on the nature of the market. If the market for the products of the assembly line in the earlier example is static, then two-thirds of the human workers may be laid off as a result of the addition of robots. However, if the market for the company's goods is growing, then adding robots to work with human beings may not lead to job losses and may even lead to hiring additional human workers, if the market is growing fast enough.

Most consumers in the future, as in the present, will live outside America's borders. For that reason, of the two sectors distinguished by economists—the traded sector and the non-traded sector—the traded sector is the most important in economic growth.

The traded sector includes industries whose goods or services can be exported to places far from where they are produced, in the same nation or in foreign countries. Examples include manufacturing and international insurance services. The non-traded sector includes industries whose goods or services must be consumed at or near where they are produced. Examples include personal services like haircuts and residential and commercial construction.

Because of the greater possibilities for growing sales in distant markets, traded sector industries are the major engines of both output growth and productivity growth in an industrial economy. Consider a metro area that has an automobile parts supplier and a hair salon. As the global middle class develops and hundreds of millions of new customers buy cars and trucks, the sales of the auto parts supplier to global automobile companies can grow dramatically. The auto parts supplier acts as a siphon for profits from around the world, some of which will spill over into adjacent industries that enrich the local economy, like other suppliers and warehouses and transportation and insurance and skills training and design. In contrast to the growing global automobile market, the market for the local hair salon's services is limited to consumers within driving distance.

The priority of national economic development policy, therefore, must be to nurture industries with global export markets that employ national workers—not just any export industries, but high-value-added industries. Advanced semiconductors or microchips are made from metallurgical-grade gravel containing silica that is turned into silicon metal by means of chemical reactions with carbon. Refined silicon metal has far more value than raw silica, and even greater value is added by advanced foundries that convert the metal into silicon chips. Officials in charge of economic development, if they know their business, will prefer to make and export silicon chips and silicon metal, not low-value-added gravel.

Manufacturing and refining processes as a rule are easier to mechanize and automate than services like haircuts. Growing global markets can allow manufacturers to add robots and workers simultaneously. Nevertheless, in all industrial societies productivity growth tends to lead the manufacturing-dominated traded sector to shed workers to non-traded service sector jobs like hairstyling.

In the absence of government intervention, over time this would tend to produce a growing divide between a thriving, export-oriented manufacturing and traded services sector, on the one hand, and a stagnant domestic services sector, on the other, in which low productivity causes low profits and low wages. Advanced robotic factories could coexist with low-wage service sweatshops, as they do now in the United States in occupations like fast food, retail, household servant jobs, and low-end nursing care.

It is therefore necessary for the national government to supplement its fostering of export-oriented, high-value-added traded sector industries with policies to raise wages and increase productivity in the non-traded domestic service sector. Public policy can boost productivity growth in low-wage sectors by several methods.

One method is simply forcing firms in the service sector to pay higher wages, as a result of higher statutory minimum wages, government-mandated collective bargaining, or government wage board mandates. Firms will be compelled to compensate for higher wages by adopting laborsaving technology, if they are not to go out of business.

Unlike many big corporations, which can pay for product and process R&D out of their profits, most small businesses cannot afford to invest in R&D to develop laborsaving technology in their fields, and others cannot afford the cost of investing in new machines like robots or computer software. The solution is for the federal government, working with state and local governments and universities, both to fund the development of laborsaving technologies in the non-traded domestic service sector and to help finance their adoption by small businesses.

A precedent for this approach can be found in the federal role in the modernization of U.S. agriculture between the Civil War and the present. The Morrill Land Grant Collage Act of 1862, passed by Congress and signed by President Lincoln, used the proceeds from the sale of federal lands to endow state colleges. Many of these were agricultural and mechanical colleges, or A&Ms, which specialized in providing technical support to manufacturers and farmers. New crop varieties and agricultural techniques developed in the laboratories of A&Ms were introduced to American farmers by county extension agents.

Another model for boosting productivity in America's low-wage, low-productivity sectors can be found in Germany's Kreditanstalt für Wiederaufbau (KfW). Among other projects, this German development bank helps small businesses that could not afford to do so otherwise develop innovative solutions to problems they encounter. In the United States, the Manufacturing Extension Partnership, an agency of the National Institute of Standards and Technology, with centers in all fifty states, attempts to play a similar role. Robert D. Atkinson and I have proposed the creation of small business boards, which in addition to helping small and medium enterprises with R&D would allow them to enjoy economies of scale, by pooling their training expenses and engaging in joint marketing and advertising.[1]

Would boosting productivity by promoting automation in both traded sector industries and non-traded domestic service occupations lead to mass unemployment? This is unlikely, for several reasons.

Since the early years of the industrial era in the nineteenth century, fears that technology will lead to mass unemployment have never been fulfilled. Technological unemployment has been limited and transient, like that caused by the replacement of horse-drawn carriages by automobiles. Devastating mass unemployment has been caused mostly by financial crises, which are particularly likely to cause serious recessions and depressions when they spread into the real estate sector. If, in the very distant future, mass technological unemployment thanks to automation were to become a problem, then sharing the jobs that remain by mandating shorter work weeks would be more faithful to the burden-sharing ethic of a wage earner's republic than a universal basic income. Steep taxation of "trophy goods" in a well-ordered society would encourage citizens to prefer more leisure time with family and friends to working long hours to win zero-sum interpersonal status competitions.

In the absence of mass technological unemployment, expanding demand for labor in one sector can absorb labor that is shed in other sectors as a result of technology-driven productivity increases. Technological innovation can be laborsaving—allowing the same output to be produced with fewer workers—or labor-augmenting—enabling greater output per worker. On the demand side, the falling price of a particular good or service may lead consumers to purchase more of the same thing, or allow them to use the money they have saved to purchase other goods or services.

Another factor is "income-elastic demand," meaning that the demand for a good or service increases with your income. The economist Robert Fogel argued that the income elasticity of demand for health care is 1.6, meaning that for every additional dollar of income, people want $1.60 in additional health care. The reason? Health is the good that makes the enjoyment of all other goods possible, so individuals and societies as they grow richer should be expected to spend more on health, even as technology causes the prices of other goods and services to fall. For this reason, Fogel, along with another eminent economist, William Baumol, predicted that, even in the absence of excessive prices and inefficiencies on the part of medical providers, the share of advanced technological economies devoted to health care would continue to grow and this would be a good thing, not a trend to be lamented.[5]

Indeed, it is possible that high-tech health care will be as central to the advanced economies of the future as the automobile-steel-oil complex was to the industrial nations of the twentieth century. The difference between manufacturing and medicine is eroding, thanks to increasingly advanced prosthetics and genetic medicine. An economy with highly automated medical labs and production facilities and computerized services with ample, well-paid jobs for nursing aides and medical manufacturing workers would be a welcome development.

Note the difference between this positive, high-tech, high-wage future scenario and today's decaying, class-ridden, post-industrial American economy. In both scenarios there would be a long-term shift from manufacturing employment to service sector employment. But today the shift is the result primarily of the replacement of U.S. manufacturing by foreign manufacturing, not the automation of U.S. factories. In today's America, nursing aides and many other health-care workers make low wages with few benefits and uncertain schedules. But the same jobs can be good jobs capable of supporting middle-class families. The fact that they are not is the result of weak worker bargaining power in America.

A new American System, the heir to the previous American systems of Hamilton and Clay and Lincoln, of FDR and Eisenhower, would have two simultaneous objectives: increasing high-value-added manufacturing for export to global markets from American factories, and helping the mostly small firms of the non-traded domestic service sector to develop and adopt labor-saving technologies so that they can pay higher wages while maintaining or expanding their output and sales.

This strategy for national economic renewal in the United States cannot succeed without limits on the ability of U.S. corporations to engage in corporate labor arbitrage, whether by offshoring vital traded sector supply chains to low-wage foreign labor pools or by importing workers to further depress wages and worker bargaining power in the low-wage, low-productivity domestic service sector. What is needed is a combination of strategic trade and immigration in the national interest.

Strategic trade should take the form of mixed trade, with different trade rules for different economic sectors. Mixed trade would have four components, each appropriate for different purposes: selective protectionism, selective free trade, reciprocal trade, and managed trade.

Let's start with selective, strategic protectionism. Under the new rules of a global mixed trade system, countries or blocs would have complete freedom to use tariffs, subsidies, quotas, procurement policies, or any other tool of industrial policy to localize any industries they wanted to foster, regain, or protect, without requiring the approval of their trading partners or transnational agencies like the World Trade Organization. In practice, most nations and blocs would seek to ensure that critical defense supply chains, along with high-value-added suppliers in civilian industries that benefit from increasing returns to scale, were found in their territories or perhaps those of military allies.

The next element of a mixed trade system would be selective free trade in certain sectors. In a global economy based on mixed trade, free trade might largely be limited to low-value-added, labor-intensive assembly operations and to agricultural, mineral, and energy commodities that all industrial economies need but that are geographically concentrated in particular regions. For example, the United States, Europe, China, and India might all choose to protect or nationalize their own domestic microchip industries while agreeing to allow free trade in silica, from which the silicon in microchips is made; in rare earths, essential to many electronic devices; and in oil and gas, which, even if they are not used for fuel, are needed as feedstocks for chemicals and plastics and fertilizers.

Reciprocal trade would be the third element of a post-neoliberal system of national and global mixed trade. Particular countries and trade blocs could engage in trade liberalization with each other, for economic reasons or to solidify military alliances. But unlike NAFTA and the WTO, bilateral or multilateral reciprocal trade treaties would not be drafted by corporate and financial sector lobbyists to make it easy for multinational corporations to transfer production to low-wage foreign workforces. Reciprocal trade would be appropriate between economies with similar wage levels, like the United States and the EU, but not between countries with radically different wage levels.

Finally, there would be managed trade, influenced by non-economic diplomatic and military considerations. Managed trade between rich and poor countries could be used in the service of regional development or military alliances, as an alternative to profit-driven cheap-labor offshoring. And managed trade might be appropriate as a confidence-building measure among geopolitical adversaries like the United States and China, with trading privileges revoked when tensions increase and restored during periods of détente.

While a strategy of mixed trade in the traded sector would prevent corporations from offshoring industrial supply chains deemed critical by the U.S. government, in the non-traded service sector labor arbitrage by employers would be limited by immigration reforms designed to increase the workplace bargaining power of American citizen-workers and legal permanent residents or green card holders.

In addition to hurting American workers who compete with them, immigrants who work for low wages by their mere presence can retard productivity growth in the sectors in which they are employed. The former World Bank economist Frank J. Lysy has observed, "New investment [in laborsaving technology] has a cost, and if the cost of the alternative (hire more labor) is low enough, then it is more profitable for the firm simply to hire more labor. Productivity in such a case will then not go up, and indeed may go down. But this could be the economically wise choice, if labor is cheap enough."[6]

In the United States, of an estimated 8 million illegal immigrants in the workforce, 1.4 million are in the construction industry, accounting for more than one in ten jobs—38 percent of drywallers, 32 percent of roofers, and 23 percent of general construction workers.[7] The reliance of the American building industry on cheap, non-union, easily intimidated illegal immigrant labor undoubtedly explains the construction sector's technological backwardness and the slow introduction of innovations like prefabricated parts and highly automated rapid prototyping or 3-D printing of entire buildings.

An example of how mass low-wage immigration can actually reverse technological progress is provided by Britain, the original homeland of the Industrial Revolution. In the British carwash industry, between 2006 and 2016 the number of automated car washes fell by half, while the number of hand car washes exploded. The British journalist Paul Mason writes, "A car wash used to mean a machine. Now it means five guys with rags. . . . The free-market economic model, combined with a globalised labour market, has produced a kind of reverse industrialisation."[8]

Just as low wages can reverse mechanization, so can high

wages stimulate it. The economist John R. Hicks, in *The Theory of Wages* (1932), described how innovation could be induced by rising wages.[9] The Habakkuk thesis is the proposal by the economist John Habakkuk that high wages caused by labor scarcity in the nineteenth-century United States encouraged American industrialization.[10] While historians debate the Habakkuk thesis, the positive effect of restricting the supply of low-wage immigrant workers on the productivity of U.S. agribusiness is well documented in recent history. Following the abolition in 1964 of the Bracero program by the Johnson administration, which had allowed half a million seasonal farmworkers to migrate from Mexico to the United States, growers responded by investing in labor-saving technologies and changing crop mixes.[11] After the state of Arizona cracked down on the employment of illegal immigrants in 2016, one Arizona grower responded by investing $2 million in developing machinery that could remove stems from jalapeno peppers, while seeking to replace unskilled farmworkers with skilled machinists.[12]

In 2020–2022, the two lowest-wage occupations—retail workers and leisure-hospitality workers—enjoyed real wage growth for the first time in many years, thanks to a tight labor market that resulted from factors including reduced immigration and "the great resignation" of dissatisfied workers that accompanied and followed the COVID-19 pandemic.[13] Tight labor markets in today's low-wage sectors, forcing employers and customers to pay more for wages, should be deliberately created by restricting the immigration of unskilled, low-wage workers.

As the failure of Cesar Chavez's United Farm Workers demonstrates, attempts to raise wages and increase worker power in low-wage occupations will fail if employers are allowed to substitute illegal immigrants for authorized workers, including legal immigrants. The focus of enforcement should be on lawbreaking employers who hire illegal immigrants, knowingly or negligently. If some employers are prosecuted to the full extent of the law, other employers will stop hiring and word will spread worldwide that you can no longer sneak into the United States or overstay your visa, buy forged credentials from criminals, and obtain jobs. When the demand by employers for illegal immigrant labor dries up, so will much of the supply. Until there is a bipartisan commitment to reducing illegal immigration from all sources to a trickle, mainly by means of employer sanctions, and until that policy has succeeded for many years, another amnesty for foreign nationals who have broken U.S. immigration laws like the one in the 1980s that was sabotaged by employers should not even be considered.

Immigration reform in the national interest also would require Congress to abolish indentured-servant/guest-worker programs in all fields, except for a few relatively insignificant occupations, like visiting professors or orchestra conductors working briefly in the United States. The H-2B agricultural guest worker program should be abolished, to force growers to raise wages or invest in laborsaving machinery. The H-1B program that has been abused by the tech and finance industries also should be abolished. Instead of being leased as employer-bound serfs to U.S. corporations by sleazy American or foreign "body shop" labor contractors, skilled immigrants should be selected by the federal government by means of a merit system of the kind used in Canada and other countries, which awards points to applicants based on their education, proficiency in English, and unlikelihood of needing public assistance.

To prevent a points-based merit system from being used by employers in labor arbitrage strategies to the detriment of American workers and the immigrants themselves, there must be overall annual numerical limits to the number of skilled immigrants, and perhaps also limits to the number of skilled immigrants any single firm can hire. Business-backed proposals to "staple a green card to every diploma" that is awarded to a foreign student must be rejected. America's corrupt and money-hungry universities admit many foreign students only because their wealthy parents are able to pay full tuition. The federal government, on the basis of objective criteria approved by Congress, should choose which foreign nationals are given the privilege of joining the American workforce and the American citizenry—not scheming corporations seeking pliant labor, and not venal universities auctioning diplomas to rich foreign families.

In the words of Barbara Jordan, the chair of President Bill Clinton's commission on immigration reform: "The commission finds no national interest in continuing to import lesser-skilled and unskilled workers to compete in the most vulnerable parts of our labor force. Many American workers do not have adequate job prospects. We should make their task easier to find employment, not harder."[14]

Limits on the offshoring of critical traded sector industries and immigration reforms that prevent employers from exploiting immigrants as pawns in wage-suppressing, union-busting labor arbitrage schemes are necessary, but not sufficient, conditions for the restoration of worker power in the United States. How to rebuild organized labor in America as a key member in a new labor-business-government partnership for American prosperity is the subject of the next chapter.

CHAPTER ELEVEN

How to Restore Worker Power in America

In the previous chapter, I made the case for a new American System based on the principles of national developmentalism and promoted by strategic trade and immigration in the national interest. If it was successful, such a strategy would restore or increase America's market share in many global industries in the traded sector while increasing productivity in the non-traded domestic service sector.

But even if a new American economic strategy of national developmentalism that replaced the failed strategy of globalist neoliberalism was to succeed, the gains from national economic growth would not necessarily be shared with America's working-class majority. Firms in both the traded and the non-traded sectors must be compelled to share their profits equitably with workers, by pressure from organized labor, government mandates, or a combination of both.

The near destruction of organized labor in the American private sector has cleared the way for innovative approaches to strengthening worker power in the aftermath of neoliberalism. In this chapter I will argue that the system of enterprise-based collective bargaining created by the National Labor Relations Act of 1935 (the Wagner Act) cannot and should not be revived. In its place three new systems to bolster the collective and individual power of workers should be considered.

In the traded sector, with its many large manufacturing firms, as well as in infrastructure and logistics industries, which tend to be dominated by natural monopolies and oligopolies, the United States needs a national system of sectoral bargaining among representatives of organized labor and organized business of the kind that exists in other democracies that treat their workers better. Sectoral bargaining on a national scale exists already in the United States under the Railway Labor Act of 1926, which covers railroad, transit, and airline employees. The Railway Labor Act system has flourished, even as the more familiar post-1935 Wagner Act system that requires each factory or warehouse or restaurant in a large corporation to be unionized has been effectively destroyed in the private sector by employer opposition. The example of the Railway Labor Act suggests that in some parts of the economy, it is possible to devise similar systems of collective bargaining in the United States at the level of the entire industry, rather than the isolated enterprise.

At the other extreme in the economy are small businesses, particularly low-profit service sector firms that pay low wages and offer no benefits to their workers. Here the alternative to sectoral collective bargaining can be found in wage boards, also called worker standard boards. For more than a century, wage boards have been used to raise wages and standards in "sweated trades" in which unionization is not realistic. In place of collective bargaining, individuals who represent labor, business, and government, and sometimes consumers, can be appointed or elected to a commission that sets standards for an entire sector like fast-food services. Wage boards need not be national in scope; they can be effective at the state or municipal level.

Rome was not built in a day, and worker power in the United States will not be rebuilt in a decade or even a generation. Pro-worker reforms should be piecemeal and incremental. The gradual extension of national sectoral bargaining in concentrated, high-tech industries should be accompanied by the steady increase over time of state or local wage boards in low-productivity, low-wage sectors like fast food, retail, and low-end health care. Meanwhile, successful sectoral bargaining and wage board strategies would leave many or most workers in other sectors without formal labor representation of any kind, at least at first. These workers, including many middle-class professionals, could be helped by a third approach: legislative reform that shifts the balance of bargaining power in employment contracts away from employers and toward American workers, by outlawing at-will employment, non-compete clauses, no-poach agreements, mandatory arbitration, and other practices used by businesses to minimize worker power in the absence of collective representation.

The combination of these three policies—sectoral collective bargaining by organized labor in concentrated industries, wage and standard setting by tripartite labor-business-government wage boards in decentralized service occupations, and legislation to strengthen basic worker rights could help to restore worker bargaining power in the twenty-first-century United States, even as the defeated and defective Wagner Act system is allowed to wither away. Only such a restoration of worker power can ensure that all Americans will have a share of the gains from a new economic strategy of national development in a new American System.

Frances Perkins, the secretary of labor under President Franklin Delano Roosevelt, is famous for remarking, "I would rather pass a law than organize a union."[1] Samuel Gompers, the founding president of the American Federation of Labor, disagreed. Gompers, who began his career as a leader of cigar-making workers, grew skeptical of reform by legislation after the New York Supreme Court overturned two laws he had helped to pass in the 1880s. As his biography on the AFL-CIO website notes, "Gompers saw that what the state gave, it could also take away."[2] Although he continued to support some legislative reforms, Gompers wanted the conditions of working men and women in the United

States to be improved chiefly as the result of negotiations between particular workers in particular industries and their employers.

Gompers favored "pure and simple unionism" that avoided political partisanship and focused narrowly on achieving a few objectives for workers and kept a safe distance between organized labor and political parties. He rejected the idea of a labor party in the United States, whether in the form of the Socialist Party or the Democratic Party. While the Democratic Party was more favorable to organized labor in the twentieth century, labor was never more than one of a number of elements in the Democratic coalition, and at its height some private sector labor unions awarded their support to sympathetic Republican elected officials. As Gompers declared in a speech in 1896 warning unions away from an embrace of the Populist Party, "The industrial field is littered with more corpses of organizations destroyed by the damning influence of partisan political action than from all other causes combined. . . . Let the watchword be: No political party domination over the trade unions; no political party influence over trade union action."[3]

Unfortunately, by 2000 the rapidly shrinking American labor movement, including the dominant public sector unions and the vestigial private sector unions, was wholly subordinated to the Democratic Party. The Democratic Party, in turn, was dominated by affluent white progressives and rich donors from Silicon Valley, Wall Street, and Hollywood who were socially liberal but often anti-union. What survives of traditional organized labor in the United States is dominated by public sector workers like unionized schoolteachers and civil servants, not private sector workers.

Traditional working-class concerns have been yoked to those of college-educated progressive activists in various single-issue movements based in the nonprofit sector and academic leftism: sexual and reproductive rights, environmentalism, racial identity politics. For example, the Clean Slate for Worker Power, a project of Harvard Law School's Labor and Worklife Program, among numerous excellent ideas for strengthening the bargaining power of American workers includes the radical proposal that in some cases employers should be required to bargain not only with representatives of labor but also with nonprofit community organizations: "For example, the worker organization would be empowered to bring community environmental justice groups to bargain over pollution controls and abatement and to bring housing groups and tenant unions to bargain over affordable housing development." Gompers would have been appalled and alarmed by the assertion that collective bargaining should include left-wing nonprofits like "environmental justice groups" that are answerable not to workers but to their funders, like progressive foundations and rich individual donors.[4]

As of this writing, the Twitter feed of Liz Shuler, the successor of Gompers as president of the AFL-CIO, has this pinned tweet: "Access to health care without fear and intimidation is every person's right. We must be able to control our own bodies—which has a direct impact on economic justice and the ability of working people to make a better life for themselves and their families."[5] The fact that the heir to Samuel Gompers makes it clear that workers whose views on abortion differ from those of the left wing of the Democratic Party are unwelcome in the AFL-CIO demonstrates the political captivity of American organized labor in its decline.

The politicization of the U.S. labor movement repels many American workers who might otherwise support it. According to one poll, the most common reason given by workers who reject union representation is not fear of retaliation by employers but union involvement in politics. When asked about progressive political issues highlighted by the AFL-CIO and SEIU, including racial justice, gender equality, and student debt forgiveness, majorities of potential union members in the poll said they did not want unions to speak out on any of these topics.[6]

Along with his fear of the capture of organized labor by political parties, the preference of Gompers for collective bargaining over top-down government legislation made sense in his time and makes sense in ours. Like Gompers, European labor leaders have often preferred negotiations with employers over one-size-fits-all labor laws. For example, in Britain and Germany and other European countries, there was no national minimum wage until recently, because none was needed. Unions negotiated living wages in many or most sectors, and wage boards or worker standards boards set decent minimums in others. It was only in the twenty-first century that the rise of an American-style "precariat" of low-income, non-union workers, swollen in part by mass low-wage immigration, made national minimum wages necessary to limit how far employers could push wages down. Britain's first national minimum wage went into effect in 1999, and Germany first adopted a national minimum wage in 2015.

In this chapter, I will argue that Frances Perkins was mostly wrong and Samuel Gompers was mostly right. If the goal is to ensure that every American has not only a living wage but also a decent job, then it is better to organize a union—or appoint a wage board—than to pass a law. But the Perkins approach of direct legislation on behalf of workers should prevail in sectors in which the Gompers approach to ensuring a living wage and decent working conditions by negotiation is impractical.

At first glance, the minimum wage might seem to support the case for the Perkins approach rather than the Gompers approach to labor issues. The U.S. minimum wage was last raised in 2009, to $7.25 an hour—far below its peak, in inflation-adjusted 2019 dollars, of $10.15 an hour ($1.60) in 1968. From its establishment by the Fair Labor Standards Act (FLSA) of 1938 until 1968, minimum-wage increases closely tracked economy-wide productivity growth. Had the minimum wage continued to rise with productivity growth, in 2024 it would be $22.19 an hour (in 2019 dollars).[7] A minimum-wage worker in 2022 made $5,000 less a year in inflation-adjusted dollars.[8]

The "Fight for $15" movement nationwide seeks to remedy

this problem. An increase in the minimum wage is popular in the United States. In 2021, according to the Pew Research Center, 62 percent of Americans supported raising the minimum wage to $15 an hour, with views divided by economic class. Seventy-two percent of lower-income people supported it, while only 55 percent of upper-income respondents did.[9]

The claim of cheap-labor lobbies and libertarian ideologues that raising the federal minimum wage moderately over time will cause mass unemployment can be dismissed. The only episodes of mass unemployment in American economic history have resulted from financial crises, like the ones that produced the Great Depression of the 1930s and the Great Recession of the 2010s, not minimum-wage increases. Nevertheless, it is undeniable that raising the minimum wage too high would lead either to large-scale unemployment or to large-scale evasion of the excessive minimum wage by employers paying workers off the books.

Even more challenging are the great disparities in the cost of living in the United States, a continental country with the third-largest national population in the world, after China and India. According to the Living Wage Calculator created by Dr. Amy K. Glasmeier of the Massachusetts Institute of Technology, a "living wage" for a single, childless adult in Grand Forks, North Dakota, would be $14.98 an hour, compared with $22.71 in New York City. New York State has a state minimum wage of $15.00 an hour. *The living wage in Grand Forks would be below the local minimum wage in New York City.*[10]

A national one-size-fits-all approach is also misguided in the case of working hours. The forty-hour week and eight-hour day were based on factory and mine labor, at a time when those sectors accounted for a much higher percentage of U.S. employment. Today most Americans—and most of the lowest paid—work in a wide variety of domestic service sector occupations. And an increasing number of professionals and managers are telecommuting from home. It makes no sense for a single set of hours and overtime rules adopted nearly a century ago to be applied to childcare workers and affluent financial industry consultants working from home offices with scenic mountain views.

As tempting as it is to try to help low-income workers directly, by means of a single high federal minimum wage of $15 an hour or for that matter $20 an hour, it is better to address low wages and bad working conditions by more flexible methods that allow more input by representatives of labor and business.

In traded sector industries like manufacturing, any effective system of selective industrial localization must be national, to ensure that state and local governments are unable to compete with one another in a race to the bottom to lure national or global factories or headquarters by lowering the wages or crippling the bargaining power of manufacturing workers. The federal government cannot prevent state and local governments from setting different tax rates under our federal constitution. That is all to the good, because a continental country like the United States with a third of a billion people cannot be governed from the center by a consolidated, unitary state.

The federal government can, however, reduce the temptation of revenue-hungry state and local governments to shower subsidies on corporations in contests with other state and local governments, by adopting a system of federal revenue sharing. Most other democratic countries have a system of fiscal equalization in which the national government collects tax revenue and redistributes it among lower-level governments, on the basis of one or another formula. The United States had its own system of general revenue sharing between 1972 and 1986, which sent federal funds to state and local governments. Proposed in the Kennedy-Johnson years and enacted under President Richard Nixon, federal revenue sharing enjoyed the support of politicians as diverse as Ronald Reagan, Hubert Humphrey, and Barry Goldwater. Unfortunately, it was eliminated in the name of deficit reduction in the Tax Reform Act of 1986.[11]

Most state and local governments used federal revenue sharing to fund schools, roads, police and emergency response departments, and other public goods. Inasmuch as funding the same public goods is the purpose of using bribes to lure corporations to their jurisdictions, the incentives to take part in bidding wars for corporate investment, to the enrichment of the companies and the detriment of state and local taxpayers, might be reduced by direct federal funding for those public services.

When it comes to labor laws and the minimum wage, federal authority is already paramount, in the form of the FLSA, the

Wagner Act, and the Railway Labor Act. The federal government should use its authority to create a system of sectoral bargaining at the national level for globally traded industries like manufacturing. If wages in particular crafts or industries are set by national collective bargaining, then the ability of state governments to lure corporations with low or nonexistent state minimum wages, on top of the federal minimum wage, will be irrelevant.

The same considerations that should govern the organization of collective bargaining in the traded sector also apply to the organization of labor in the high-value-added non-traded infrastructure sector. Wages and hours and benefits in regional and national infrastructure grids and networks that cross state lines should be set by sectoral bargaining at the federal level.

As it happens, both criteria are met by the Railway Labor Act of 1926, which, as noted earlier, includes airline workers and transit workers as well as railroad workers. Unlike the Wagner Act, the Railway Labor Act provides no barriers to national, multiemployer collective bargaining.

In the most recent 2020 national bargaining round in the railroad industry, the National Carriers' Conference Committee, representing thirty-seven railroads, including CSX and Union Pacific, negotiated with twelve rail unions that represent roughly 125,000 employees.[12] In the fall of 2022, President Biden and Congress intervened to impose a deal on railroad companies and workers under the auspices of the Railway Labor Act.

The contrast between industries covered by the failed Wagner Act of 1935 and those covered by the Railway Labor Act is striking, in terms of both union density and coverage. In 2018, 81 percent of subway, train, and rail workers were covered by union agreements, and 77 percent were unionized. According to the Bureau of Labor Statistics, even though the typical entry-level credential of a railroad worker is a high school diploma or equiv-alent, the median pay of railroad workers in 2018 was $61,480 per year. In contrast, in transportation and warehousing, defined by BLS as "private-sector industries with high unionization," only 16.1 percent of workers were unionized. Truck drivers make $47,000 a year, and school bus drivers only $34,820.[13]

The Railway Labor Act could serve as a model for national sectoral bargaining in other concentrated industries. Alternately, rather than try to invent an entirely new system of national sec-toral bargaining, it might be worth updating and extending the Railway Labor Act to include both new transportation indus-tries, such as trucking and taxis, private infrastructure industries including warehouses like those of Amazon and FedEx, and defense-critical manufacturing, which like critical infrastructure and transportation can be defined as essential to national secu-rity. Over time automation is likely to reduce the number of work-ers in railroads, trucking, and manufacturing, while deepening the interaction of these sectors, so adding more workers in highly automated industries would not necessarily be highly burdensome and might even promote productivity growth.

Decoupling coverage from union membership would make it

unnecessary to unionize particular companies or particular factories, warehouses, or other establishments. In France, fewer than
10 percent of workers belong to labor unions, but most workers
in most occupations are covered by sectoral collective bargaining
agreements. In the United States, the goal should be expanding the number of workers covered by collective bargaining without necessarily expanding the number of workers who belong to
unions.

A different approach is needed in the low-wage service sectors of the U.S. economy, where worker interests can be
defended best by wage boards.

The problem of employers who pay their workers too little to
live on is as old as the industrial era. In 1909, a young, ambitious
member of the British House of Commons explained why he was
introducing a bill to address the problem of geographically dis-
persed, low-wage work:

> The same evils exist in other industrial countries—France,
> Germany, Austria, and the United States of America.... The
> trade becomes a parasitic trade, feeding upon other industries
> and trades in the country and on the wealth of the nation, for
> in such a case the wages bill of the sweated industry is largely
> paid by the relatives with whom the worker lives, by the poor
> law, by the community who subscribe to hospitals and asylums,

by charity, and by a proportion of the cost of old age pensions.

I think I may say that such a trade is a parasitic trade.

The young politician argued that the best way to prevent society in general—"the relatives," "the poor law," and "charity"—from indirectly subsidizing "parasitic" low-wage employers by rescuing their workers from poverty was for the government to establish trade boards. Now known as wage boards or worker standards boards, these trade board commissions would set minimum wages and other standards for all of the workers in particular low-wage occupations.

Asked whether increasing the wages of impoverished workers would increase prices, the sponsor of the bill acknowledged that it might, but pointed out that there were many ways that employers could alter their business models to minimize the effect of higher wages, and noted that higher wages can stimulate technological innovation: "Well, again, I should like to remind the House that an increase of wages brings increased efficiency, and increased efficiency brings an increase not only in quality but in quantity. There is, no doubt, that it further stimulates resource on the part of manufacturers and the inventive genius of the people who give their minds to mechanics."[14]

The name of the bill was the Trade Boards Act of 1909, and the young member of the House of Commons who sponsored it was Winston Churchill.[15]

In the United States, a short-lived federal wage board system was created in 1938 by the Fair Labor Standards Act, which established today's minimum wage, maximum hours, and overtime laws. The FLSA initially created federal wage boards or "industry committees" with tripartite representation of unions, employers, and the public that were authorized to set minimum wages (though not working conditions or benefits) in particular industries. In 1949, however, during a backlash against pro-labor laws led by segregationist Democrats and anti–New Deal Republicans, the FLSA was amended to eliminate the tripartite federal wage boards, except in the cases of Puerto Rico and the Virgin Islands.[16]

A few states, including New York, California, New Jersey, and Arizona, have statutes authorizing tripartite wage boards to set wages or regulations in specific industries that date back to the early twentieth century. Other states allow the executive branch, following public hearings, to regulate wages or hours in specific occupations.[17]

Using a law passed in 1933, Governor Andrew Cuomo ordered the state labor commissioner to convene a wage board that would make recommendations for wages in the poorly paid restaurant sector.[18] The three-member commission, made up of a business executive, a labor union leader, and a former county executive, undertook investigations and ultimately raised the minimum wage for hourly fast-food workers from $8.75 to $15.00 an hour over several years. New York also authorized a wage board for farmworkers in 2019.[19] The successful experiment has inspired efforts in other states.

The federal government should use subsidies and legal waivers to promote the creation of a federal-state wage board system in all fifty states and the District of Columbia. To this end, the FLSA could be amended to create a Fair Labor Standards Commission (FLSC). To prevent excessive partisanship and ensure stability and continuity of policy, the FLSC should not be housed in an executive agency directly subordinate to the White House and controlled by presidential appointees. Instead, like the Federal Communications Commission and the Federal Trade Commission, the Federal Labor Standards Commission should be organized as an independent agency, led by a multimember commission with staggered terms and a strong norm or legal requirement that both major parties be represented among the commissioners. The Fair Labor Standards Commission might be empowered to grant businesses in a particular occupation or industry in a state waivers from one or more FLSA rules, in return for the state's creation of a wage board whose rules bind all businesses in that occupation or industry.

Various incentives might be used to overcome the resistance of some businesses, particularly small businesses, to state wage board rule making. One option might be to combine the wage boards with other innovative agencies that help small businesses in particular sectors boost their productivity, as Robert D. Atkinson and I have proposed.[20] The goal of industrial policy in non-traded sectors like retail, janitorial services, maid service, and construction should be to raise wages by labor policy while at the same time raising sector-wide productivity by sector-specific methods.

Many if not most American workers, at least at first, would not be covered either by national sectoral bargaining, based in the big-firm national manufacturing and infrastructure sector, or by wage boards, which initially would focus on the occupations with the lowest wages and the worst jobs. These unrepresented individual workers could be helped by reforms in employment law that shifted power away from employers toward workers, like the elimination of most at-will employment, most non-compete agreements, no-poach agreements, and mandatory arbitration clauses in employment contracts.

At the moment, it may seem utopian to think that widespread coverage by wage and work rules negotiated by either labor unions or wage boards can ever exist in the U.S. private sector. There is no doubt that most American employers will fight to defend the present system of almost unlimited employer autocracy and worker powerlessness. Even attempts to change unfair labor practices like non-compete clauses meet savage resistance from employers who profit by mistreating their workers.

But maintaining the anti-worker status quo in the United States may not be an option in the future. The pulverization of private sector unions, the dependence of both national parties on rich individual donors and corporations and banks, and the domination of politics by affluent professionals, managers, and small business owners have left most working-class Americans with nobody to turn to apart from occasional would-be tribunes of the masses like Bernie Sanders or Donald Trump. In the decades and generations to come, American national politics may see the rise of more dangerous demagogues along the lines of Louisiana's Huey Long or Argentina's Juan Perón.

If that comes to pass, then corporate America might regret its dismissal of institutions like wage boards and multiemployer collective bargaining at the sectoral level and federal legislation to strengthen the bargaining power of individual workers. The future equivalents of Samuel Gompers and Frances Perkins would be easier for American firms to do business with than the future equivalents of Huey Long.

CHAPTER TWELVE

"Keep Your Government Hands Off My Medicare"

Social Insurance and the Work Ethic

To avert economic and social decline, the United States must transition from a low-wage/high-welfare system to a living-wage/social-insurance economy—that is the argument of this book. With few exceptions, no full-time worker should need to rely on means-tested public assistance, whether in the form of wage subsidies like the earned income tax credit, food stamps, or housing vouchers. The paychecks of all workers should be adequate for two kinds of costs: the recurrent costs of shelter, food, clothing, transportation, and other necessities for workers and their families; and the cost of contributions or premiums like payroll taxes that pay for a system of income maintenance during periods of unemployment caused by retirement, illness, disability, temporary joblessness, or the need to provide family care. All of the ordinary worker's needs should be paid for by the employer, with the cost either coming out of reduced employer profits or passed along to the consumer in the form of higher prices.

The living-wage/social-insurance approach to organizing a modern technological, urban society of wage earners has affinities with the ethic of small-*r* republicanism. In a democratic republic, the dependence of citizens on employers and on the state should be minimized. In an industrial republic whose economy is based on mass production and specialization, unlike in an agrarian republic, the ideal of personal and family independence cannot be achieved by means of widespread ownership of farms and small businesses. Most citizens in an industrial economy have to sell their labor to private, public, and nonprofit employers, in return for a wage.

Nevertheless, even in a republic of wage earners a kind of economic independence from employers can be obtained, if the workers abandon the obsolete agrarian-era ethic of individual self-reliance and collaborate with one another. By joining forces in collective bargaining, workers can raise their wages in unison, and by pooling some of their resources, they can insure one another against unemployment, sickness, disability, and temporary absence from the workforce to provide family care.

For those attracted to the ideal of a wage earner's republic, the low-wage/high-welfare system of the contemporary United States is a dystopian nightmare. Lacking representation by organized labor, the poorest-paid workers cannot live on their below-poverty wages. They must rely on means-tested public assistance or welfare, as a condition of which they must take any job available—*including jobs that pay poverty wages.* Thus the low-wage job creates welfare dependency, and the welfare state encourages low-wage work. Inevitably, this system creates a two-tier labor force, with an underclass of workers who derive part of their income from employers and part from means-tested welfare programs. Some workers can be trapped for their entire lives under the joint control of exploitative employers and punitive welfare bureaucrats, and their serf-like status—incompatible with the pride and self-reliance of the citizen of a republic, even a wage earner's republic—can be passed along to their descendants. The desperate efforts of the majority of citizens to escape the ranks of the welfare-dependent working poor by engaging in a credential arms race sets off a chain reaction of social pathologies in areas from family life to national politics, as we have seen.

In the previous chapter I made the case for a living wage, preferably as the result of negotiation among organized workers and organized employers rather than benevolent legislation by a paternalistic political elite. In this chapter I will make the case for mutual insurance among wage earners, in the form of government-mediated social insurance, as the complement to a living wage. When combined, a living wage and a comprehensive system of social insurance benefits earned by work can restore the bargaining power that American workers in the last half century have lost.[1]

During a town hall meeting in 2009 in Simpsonville, South Carolina, convened by Representative Robert Inglis (R—S.C.) during the debate over what became the Affordable Care Act (Obamacare), a constituent told Inglis to "keep your government hands off my Medicare." According to Inglis, "I had to politely explain that, 'Actually, sir, your health care is being provided by the government.' . . . But he wasn't having any of it."[2]

Having been mocked by his own congressional representative, the anonymous voter was ridiculed in the national media. Pundits across the political spectrum seized on the remark to symbolize the lamentable ignorance of ordinary people in general and populist conservatives in particular. On the right, the libertarian economist Tyler Cowen called the voter's statement "the funniest sentence I read today."[3] On the left, *Slate*'s Timothy Noah announced an initiative "to combat the pernicious and big-babyish meme that Medicare lies beyond government control and must remain so."[4]

With its supercilious mockery, the overclass intelligentsia of left, right, and center revealed an inability to distinguish between *public assistance* and *social insurance*, which both market fundamentalists on the right and socialists on the left regard as interchangeable for ideological reasons. The market fundamentalist evaluates public programs on the starkly utilitarian basis of how much monetary value flows to whom, without regard to moral justification.

The socialist obsesses over moral justification but embraces a framework in which all are equally deserving of public support. To both groups, then, money is money, whatever its source. People pay the taxes they can afford and receive the benefits they need.

Most Americans think otherwise. Along with citizens of other modern democracies, they see a profound moral and political difference between noncontributory public assistance paid out of general tax revenues ("welfare") and contributory social insurance funded by payroll taxes or premiums ("earned benefits"), even if both kinds of programs involve government spending. Medicare may be *administered* by the government, but it is a program of, by, and for the working people who pay for and receive it.

Underlying this disconnect in thinking about the welfare state is a debate between two moral systems, which might be called the work ethic and the consumption ethic. The work ethic views membership in a community as entailing a reciprocal obligation to contribute through personal effort—whether paid or unpaid—to the community's flourishing, rather than exploiting others by free riding on their efforts. The consumption ethic in contrast views work as merely a means to the end of personal consumption, with no intrinsic value to distinguish it from other sources of income that allow for enjoyment of the same consumer goods—private charity, government welfare, or capital gains derived from the passive ownership of assets that generate profits, rents, or interest.

For the typical worker in modern urban, industrial economies, wages have always been too low to permit saving in advance for all possible emergencies. Instead, the sensible and highly valued option for wage earners is to acquire insurance against unlikely and unaffordable costs like a health crisis, on the one hand, and the prospect of income loss from unemployment or disability, on the other. An annuity provides insurance against poverty during retirement in old age. In some instances, insurance products for these purposes are available for purchase in the commercial market. But in many other cases, private insurance markets make provision implausible or prohibitively expensive for many or most wage earners.

One response in the early industrial era was the development by workers themselves of "friendly societies" or nonprofit mutual aid societies. These membership organizations, often with colorful names like the Ancient Order of Foresters or the Odd Fellows or the Shriners (Freemasons), combined the functions of modern insurance in cases of sickness, burial costs, old-age assistance, and other expenses with the social activities of modern guilds, like regular feasting and parades. But many workers could not afford to pay dues, and nonprofit mutual aid societies often excluded people in poor health or poor financial condition to avoid adverse selection, just as commercial insurers did.

Social insurance works well only if participation is universal or near universal, which in many cases necessitates state-compelled membership in contributory systems. If paying premiums is voluntary, then the exit of the affluent and young can create a death spiral into insolvency for social insurance, just as for commercial insurance, where a dwindling number of sick and elderly people can face ever-higher premiums. For this reason, most industrial nations with wage-earning majorities have adopted systems of social insurance administered by the state (although relics of mutual aid societies survive in the German sickness funds and the Ghent system of union-administered benefits in Sweden and the Czech Republic).

The divide between the work ethic and the consumption ethic has yielded competing visions for social insurance: the Bismarck-ian and the Beveridgean. The Bismarckian model, named after the chancellor of imperial Germany who pioneered the modern welfare state to weaken the appeal of socialism to the working class, is modeled on private insurance. Bismarckian social insur-ance is based on contributory taxes, usually payroll taxes, and workers who contribute more may receive higher benefits.

The rival model of social insurance is named after the British liberal economist William Beveridge, whose November 1942 re-port set forth the Beveridge Plan for the postwar British welfare state, a vision never completely realized in the U.K. or elsewhere. In the Beveridgean model, public payments for health care, pub-lic pensions, unemployment insurance, and the like come out of general taxes, similar to spending on defense or infrastructure or public education.

The American social insurance and assistance programs es-tablished by the New Deal in the 1930s—Social Security, unem-ployment insurance, disability insurance, and Aid to Dependent Children (ADC)—for the most part reflected the Bismarckian model and embodied the work ethic by creating earned benefits with eligibility based on a history of work and payroll tax contributions. ADC was designed explicitly as a program for the deserving poor on the work ethic model of social assistance, targeting widows with children in an era that took the assumption of a male breadwinner for granted.

Twenty-first-century progressives who think they are in the tradition of the New Deal Democrats while defining social justice as more unconditional cash aid to citizens are in for a shock if they read President Franklin Delano Roosevelt's 1935 State of the Union address. In words that eloquently express the work ethic, FDR called for the abolition of cash aid for the unemployed and its replacement by public sector jobs:

> A large proportion of these unemployed and their dependents have been forced on the relief rolls. The burden on the Federal Government has grown with great rapidity. We have here a human as well as an economic problem. When humane considerations are concerned, Americans give them precedence. The lessons of history, confirmed by the evidence immediately before me, show conclusively that continued dependence upon relief induces a spiritual disintegration fundamentally destructive to the national fiber. To dole out relief in this way is to administer a narcotic, a subtle destroyer of the human spirit. It is inimical to the dictates of a sound policy. It is in violation of the traditions of America. Work must be found for able-bodied but destitute workers.

> The Federal Government must and shall quit this business of relief.
>
> I am not willing that the vitality of our people be further sapped by the giving of cash, of market baskets, of a few hours of weekly work cutting grass, raking leaves, or picking up papers in the public parks. We must preserve not only the bodies of the unemployed from destitution but also their self-respect, their self-reliance, and courage and determination.[5]

President Roosevelt explained his preference for a contributory social-insurance system to Luther Gulick, an economist who advised the federal government, in the summer of 1941. When Gulick, like many economists then and now, complained that the payroll tax was a regressive tax on workers, FDR replied,

> I guess you're right on the economics. They are politics all the way through. We put those pay roll contributions there so as to give the contributors a legal, moral, and political right to collect their pensions and their unemployment benefits. With those taxes in there, no damn politician can ever scrap my social security program. Those taxes aren't a matter of economics, they're straight politics.[6]

Like Social Security, Medicare was designed to be an earned benefit based on years of work effort via payroll tax contributions. The distinction between earned benefits like Social Security and Medicare, on the one hand, and public assistance, a kind of charity, on the other hand, was central to the ethos of the New Deal and reflects the values of many if not most Americans in the twenty-first century, as it did in the twentieth. Far from mocking the individual who said, "Keep your government hands off my Medicare," FDR would have been delighted.

For decades, rich individuals like the late Pete Peterson, corporations, and banks have funded scare campaigns in the United States claiming that "entitlements" like Social Security and Medicare face bankruptcy that can only be averted if their benefits are cut. In fact, their shortfalls can be remedied by relatively modest tweaks. The real problem with America's social-insurance entitlements is that there are too few of them, not too many. It would be far more efficient for federal subsidies for children and caregivers, for example, to take the form of social-insurance benefits, along with Social Security retirement benefits and unemployment insurance, instead of clumsy and hard-to-use tax credits.

Adding several universal family benefits like a child-care benefit and a family caregiver benefit to the existing U.S. social-insurance system would somewhat increase the cost of payroll taxes for workers. This in turn will increase the cost to employers, and perhaps to consumers, of the overall compensation of each worker—the wage plus the payroll tax and the cost of other taxes and benefits. Good! The goal, remember, is to move away from the present American system, which socializes the costs of low-wage jobs while privatizing the benefits for employers and consumers of low-wage labor, toward a system in which all of the costs of workers are privatized and the taxpayer is not forced indirectly to subsidize cheap-labor employers and their customers.

The "tax wedge" is the technical term for the difference between the take-home pay of a worker and what it costs an employer to employ that worker. In the United States in 2021, the tax wedge for a single individual worker was 28.4 percent of the worker's take-home pay, compared with an average of 36.4 percent among the thirty-eight member countries of the Organization for Economic Cooperation and Development (OECD). Thanks to low wages, low payroll taxes, and miserly social-insurance benefits, the United States had the dubious distinction of having the thirtieth-lowest tax wedge among the thirty-eight OECD countries.[7]

Many Americans on the left mistakenly believe that European countries with generous social spending pay for it with extremely high taxes on the rich, when in reality the funds come largely from higher payroll taxes and higher value-added consumption taxes that fall broadly on the population as a whole. This mistake leads many American progressives to embrace mathematically impossible proposals, like promises to fund vastly expanded redistribution to the "99 percent" by soaking "the billionaires" while avoiding any tax increases on households making less than

$400,000 a year (Joe Biden, in his 2020 presidential campaign) or $200,000 a year (Hillary Clinton, in her 2016 presidential campaign).

While employers whose business models depend on low wages will fight any increase in overall compensation for their underpaid workers, whether in the form of take-home pay or payroll tax increases, it is possible to imagine a left-right compromise in favor of higher payroll taxes for expanded social-insurance benefits. In return for giving up the fantasy of paying for those benefits entirely by means of steep and unrealistic increases in taxes on the rich, the center-left might get family social-insurance benefits that are earned by work history and thus less politically vulnerable to future efforts at repeal than other policies like tax credits. For their part, pro-family conservatives would get programs designed to reinforce the work ethic, allow working parents to take pride in providing for their families, and deter free riding on public assistance. The winners would be working-class families and their children, traditional social democrats, and conservative familists. The losers would be cheap-labor employers, ideological libertarians, and those on the socialist left who reject the distinction between earned social-insurance benefits and public assistance.

The necessary increase in the cost of hiring new employees that would result from higher social-insurance payroll taxes on top of living wages might be reduced for employers by lowering corporate income taxes (which arguably should be replaced anyway by direct taxes on individuals). The cost of expanded social insurance might also be reduced by removing some taxes and premiums that are now included in the payroll tax. An ideal social-insurance system would be limited to the narrow purpose of income maintenance, redistributing money from adults in the workforce to those unable to work because they are children, caregivers of young children or other family members, temporarily unemployed, sick or disabled, or retired.

In hindsight it was a mistake to include Medicare and Medicaid in the social-insurance system, because the provision of medical care is not a form of income maintenance but a "merit good" that should be provided for all citizens, whether they can afford it or not. Health-care programs have more in common with the public provision of education, through a public school monopoly or through school choice vouchers, and with the public regulation of affordable utilities like water and electricity. From this it follows that government health-care spending should be paid for by taxes other than payroll taxes.

It might be objected that reducing or eliminating payroll tax contributions would weaken the claim of recipients of Medicare and Medicaid to health care. But all Americans except for the most sociopathic libertarians think that people who are unable to pay their household utility bills should be protected from having their water or electricity cut off, even though paying for water and electricity is not organized as a social-insurance benefit paid for by payroll taxes on work. In any event, of the four parts of Medicare, only Part A, which covers inpatient hospital stays, skilled nursing facility care, some home health visits, and hospice care, is financed primarily by a 2.9 percent combined payroll tax on employers and employees (1.5 percent each), with a somewhat higher payroll tax on higher earners. To make room for payroll taxes to pay for new family benefits, the payroll tax contribution to Medicare as a whole might be shrunk from around a third, if not entirely eliminated, and replaced by increases in the two other major taxes that pay for Medicare—general revenues and premiums—or perhaps other taxes.[8] More room for new family benefits can be created by reducing or eliminating the combined employer-employee payroll tax of 2.9 percent for Medicare.*

Even as it strengthens the bargaining power of individual members of the working class, a system of government insurance along mutualist lines reduces the dependence of the working class as a whole on the rich as a group. In practice, every system of social insurance in modern democracies involves considerable redistribution of income from affluent workers to low-income workers. But a system of social insurance should be designed so that it would be solvent, even if all of the rich in the country decided to engage in a "capital strike," renounce their U.S. citizenship, and take up new lives as expatriates in the tax haven of Belize. Social insurance should be designed for an ideal one-class

---

*The greatest problem with the U.S. health-care system is not insurance coverage but the routine price gouging that is enabled by the unchecked market power of American pharma companies, hospitals, and the MD cartel. The only effective solution—the adoption of an all-payer system for both private and public health-care providers of the kind used by most other developed countries, which would turn the U.S. health-care industry into a privately owned but price-regulated public utility—is beyond the scope of this discussion.

society in which everyone is working class, in which there is no vertical redistribution from rich to poor, but only horizontal redistribution from working-class people who are in the labor market to other working-class people who, for legitimate reasons, are out of the labor market temporarily or permanently.

Even though it is compulsory and administered by the government, social insurance, like collective bargaining, is a form of collaboration in which members of the working-class majority unite to help one another achieve shared economic security, in a modern technological economy in which the isolated individual worker cannot hope for personal economic independence and cannot count on the charity of the economic elite. In a republic of wage earners, collective bargaining and social insurance are two complementary forms of working-class solidarity.

AFTERWORD

Making America Work for American Workers

American country music has long drawn much of its subject matter from sorrowful tales of rural and blue-collar Americans who are down on their luck—or at least it did, before becoming diluted by admixture with upbeat generic pop music. An old joke has it that if you play a country music song backward, you get your wife back, your job back, your truck back, your double-wide trailer home back, and your dog back.

Those who criticize the post-1980s neoliberal regime in the United States and other Western democracies are often accused of wanting to play the record backward to get the 1950s back. Inevitably this is accompanied by taunts that critics of neoliberal globalism idealize the past and ignore the existence of racial segregation and sexism and the criminalization of homosexuality in

1950s America. If you think about it, this is a weird criticism, implying that civil rights for racial minorities, women, and gay men and lesbians necessarily come in a package with de-unionization, deindustrialization, income polarization, and low-wage jobs.

We cannot play history backward from the dystopian 2020s to the golden age of the prosperous American working class between the 1940s and the 1980s—a tarnished golden age, indeed, with institutions from which many Americans were unfairly excluded. Reshoring some critical supply chains is in America's interest for both strategic and economic reasons, but the number of Americans directly employed in manufacturing is likely to decline in the long run thanks to automation, even though automation's role in the decline of U.S. manufacturing jobs to date has been overstated. The vertically integrated corporations of the mid-twentieth century, in which rubber and steel went into one end and automobiles or refrigerators came out of the other, are no more likely to be restored than the outsourcing by firms of many jobs to arm's-length vendors is likely to be reversed.

But if the institutions of the half-century New Deal era cannot be revived, the underlying principles remain popular. Why wouldn't most Americans of all races and national origins in the twenty-first century—even young Americans who know the last century only from books—prefer the mid-twentieth-century model of organizing a modern industrial nation-state to the failed neoliberal globalist model that replaced it?

As we have seen, if we reject socialism, which at great risk makes the political bosses the economic bosses as well, there are only two basic ways to organize a modern society in which most people must survive by selling their labor for money and most productive enterprises are privately owned. One is a living-wage/social-insurance system in which wages are high enough to pay both for recurrent expenses and for social-insurance premiums so that nobody who works full time is poor and in need of means-tested public assistance. The other is a low-wage/high-welfare system in which a substantial part of the workforce, the so-called working poor, cannot survive on wages alone and depends on public assistance.

As it happens, the last century of American history illustrates both models of modified capitalism. The New Deal order from the 1930s to the 1980s was a version of the living-wage/social-insurance system. The neoliberal order of the 1980s to the 2020s has been a version of the low-wage/high-welfare system. There is no reason in theory why a living-wage/social-insurance society could not be constructed in the age of computers and the internet.

There would be costs, to be sure. But there are costs imposed by every social order. America's present low-wage system shifts the costs of ensuring the survival of low-wage workers to American taxpayers, via the welfare system. In a living-wage regime, the costs of supporting all workers would fall almost entirely on their employers and consumers. Higher wages make possible less welfare spending.

As we have seen, one response to more-expensive labor would be investment in laborsaving technology, in industries in which that is an option. Innovative technology could allow the prices of goods and services to remain the same, even as the workers who produced them earned more money.

In other occupations, however, it might not be possible to abandon labor-intensive goods production or service provision. In those cases, consumers could decide to pay more for the same good or service, or they could choose to do without it, or do it on their own. In a high-wage America, some occupations that exist only because of low wages, like masseurs in airports, would vanish altogether if the workers were paid more. Good riddance.

What about necessary labor-intensive services, like physical therapy for medical patients, as opposed to airport massages for stressed-out travelers? If these services or goods are considered "merit goods," that is, goods that should be available to all citizens regardless of ability to pay, then the government should pay for them directly or indirectly. If the government subsidizes a labor-intensive service, however, it must take care to regulate the prices as it does in the case of public utilities, to deny the ability of the providers to raise prices in response to the consumer subsidies, as U.S. universities have done in response to student loans and as U.S. medical providers have done in response to federal tax subsidies for public and private health insurance.

Critics might warn that attempts to raise wages faster than productivity growth could cause widespread inflation. Earlier I argued that in the case of low-tech, low-profit, low-wage sectors, raising wages might be for the best if it shocked reluctant employers into increasing their productivity.

That point aside, however, it is true that a high-wage economy like that of the United States before the 1980s can be afflicted by "wage-push" inflation. Wage-push inflation would be a good problem to have, after half a century of wage suppression by various means, including artificial recessions created by the U.S. Federal Reserve to throw millions of workers into unemployment, in order to terrify the rest into moderating their wage demands for fear of losing their jobs as well. A better response to wage-driven inflation, used in some other countries in the past but never in the United States, consists of "social compacts" among government, business, and organized labor, with labor agreeing to wage moderation. Cross-class collaboration to tame inflation is more likely to produce a harmonious and civilized society than the suppression of working-class power by a brutal ruling class.

There can be no doubt that, given the choice, most American voters would choose the living-wage/social-insurance model instead of the low-wage/high-welfare model. Most Americans of all races have never embraced the post-1980s neoliberal system that was imposed from above on the country by the bipartisan political elite and its backers in business and banking at the end of the twentieth century.

In 2021, 68 percent of Americans approved of labor unions. Sixty-two percent of Americans support a federal minimum wage of $15.00 an hour (today it is $7.25); among the 38 percent who oppose it, 71 percent want a more moderate increase, and only 27 percent want no increase at all.[1] Seventy-four percent of

Americans—including 68 percent of Republicans and Republican "leaners"—oppose any reductions in Social Security benefits.[2]

Nearly half a century since the American elite began promoting neoliberal globalization policies in the 1980s and 1990s, majorities of Americans reject those policies. On the verge of the passage of NAFTA by Congress in 1993, only 36 percent of respondents in an NBC–*Wall Street Journal* poll supported that transnational labor arbitrage treaty.[3] In 2021, during the Biden administration, a poll by the Chicago Council on Global Affairs showed that 57 percent of Americans favored reducing U.S. trade with China, even if that resulted in higher costs for American consumers and businesses. Sixty-two percent favored tariffs on Chinese imports. Seventy-nine percent of respondents said that protecting the jobs of American workers is a "very important" goal, ranging from 72 percent of Democrats to 76 percent of independents and 89 percent of Republicans.[4] In a 2019 poll by the Center for American Progress, the three most important U.S. foreign policy priorities chosen by respondents were "protecting against terrorist threats like ISIS or al-Qaeda" (40 percent), "protecting jobs for American workers" (36 percent), and "reducing illegal immigration" (35 percent).[5]

Speaking of illegal immigration, most Americans have opposed increasing the number even of legal immigrants as long as there have been polls on the subject. Between 1967 and 2021, no more than 33 percent of Americans has ever wanted immigration to be increased. Among the majority who have opposed increasing immigration ever since the 1960s, those who want to decrease immigration have usually outnumbered those who want total immigrant numbers to remain the same.[6]

For half a century, then, under both neoliberal globalist Democrats and neoliberal globalist Republicans, the U.S. government has promoted trade and immigration policies that have been the exact opposite of what most Americans want. And Americans have noticed. In 2021, when the Chicago Council on Global Affairs asked those whom it polled which groups benefit from U.S. foreign policy, only minorities chose "Working-class Americans" (42 percent), "Middle-class Americans" (44 percent), or "Small companies" (38 percent). The main beneficiaries of U.S. foreign policy, according to most respondents in this poll, are "Large corporations" (92 percent), "The U.S. government" (90 percent), "Wealthy Americans" (87 percent), and "The U.S. military" (80 percent).

The replacement of today's neoliberal low-wage/high-welfare system by a new living-wage/social-insurance system would be popular with most American voters, if not with America's economic elite. At the same time, a living-wage system would ameliorate if not eliminate the crises that the low-wage economy has worsened.

If all Americans could get living-wage jobs reinforced by expanded social-insurance benefits on graduating from high school, they could form families sooner and have the number of children that many women and men tell pollsters they want, instead of the smaller number they have in today's economy, in which working-class Americans postpone or forgo marriage because of financial insecurity, while elite Americans spend their twenties and sometimes their thirties in school or starting professional careers. Work and marriage and children would all bring isolated members of the working class into greater contact with others, reducing the epidemic of anomie and loneliness.

Politics, too, might be transformed for the better, if a strong foundation of good jobs with living wages and decent conditions held up the American economy. Members of a more prosperous, powerful, and confident working class would feel less need to join the credential arms race for the prizes of diplomas or occupational licenses. With fewer Americans of all races needing to attend college to obtain good jobs, identity politics—best understood as status competition within the college-educated overclass— would lose much of its fervor. And if organized labor in a new and nonpartisan form did evolve, its institutions could cause a shift away from ideology-driven hysteria toward a calmer, more pragmatic, and more transactional politics focused on the day-to-day concerns of typical working families.

Needless to say, the beneficiaries of today's neoliberal economic order will try to defend America's disastrous low-wage/ high-welfare model as inevitable, if not good. But if I have persuaded you of nothing else in this book, I hope that I have convinced you that the economic trends I have enumerated—and the harmful social trends that they inflame—cannot be sustained.

A form of capitalism that rewards firms for cutting labor costs by cutting wages instead of increasing productivity boosts short-term profits at the price of long-term decline. Firms compete to reduce national productive capacity, by offshoring or abandoning manufacturing industries that are essential to growth and national security. And because most consumers are workers whose spending depends on their wages, cheap-labor capitalism shrinks the national consumer market.

In any race to the bottom, at some point the bottom will be reached. Neoliberal globalism, an unsustainable scheme based on constant replacement of more-expensive labor by cheaper labor, like all Ponzi schemes, will come to an end and be replaced by a different social and economic order in the United States.

The post-neoliberal order may not be better. It could be worse. The emergent national class hierarchy in America may solidify into a neo-feudal system run by a more or less hereditary aristocracy that assigns everyone incomes and rewards based on government-certified identity categories like race and gender or discretionary political patronage. Another possibility is that populist demagogues, some of them perhaps more effective and focused than Donald Trump, will lead ephemeral and disruptive rebellions by the marginalized and dispossessed.[7]

Given the nightmarish alternatives of stable oligarchy or demagogue-exploited turmoil, the restoration of worker power in the United States of America is worth a try.

ACKNOWLEDGMENTS

This book grew from an essay, "The Five Crises of the American Regime," published by *Tablet* on January 7, 2021, the day after a pro-Trump mob ransacked the U.S. Capitol. Other material in this book also appeared in the magazine. I am indebted to Alana Newhouse, founder and editor in chief, and David Samuels, literary editor, for the privilege of being a contributor to *Tablet*.

I would like to express my gratitude to Julius Krein and Gladden Pappin of *American Affairs*, and to Oren Cass of American Compass, where parts of this book were previously published. In addition, I owe thanks to Anne-Marie Slaughter, CEO of New America, and Paul Butler, president of New America, for graciously allowing me to continue my affiliation as a fellow with the think tank I cofounded; and Angela Evans, dean emerita of the Lyndon B. Johnson School of Public Affairs of the University of Texas at Austin, where I taught while writing *Hell to Pay*.

Finally, I am indebted to Bria Sandford, executive editor at Portfolio, and my agent, Kristine Dahl of International Creative Management, for their guidance and support.

NOTES

FOREWORD

1. Daniel Alpert and Robert C. Hockett, "The Jobs Market Isn't as Healthy as It Seems," *Bloomberg*, December 19, 2019.

2. Occupational Employment Statistics, *May 2019 National Occupational Employment and Wage Estimates, United States*, U.S. Bureau of Labor Statistics, 2020.

3. Assistant Secretary for Planning and Evaluation, 2019 Poverty Guidelines, U.S. Department of Health and Human Services, cited in National Academy of Social Insurance, *Economic Security for the 21st Century* (Washington, D.C.: National Academy of Social Insurance, 2022).

4. Martha Ross and Nicole Bateman, "Meet the Low-Wage Workforce," Metropolitan Policy Program, Brookings Institution, November 2019, 9.

5. "1960 Census: Population, Supplementary Reports: Educational Attainment of the Population of the United States," PC(S1)-37, December 27, 1962; U.S. Census Bureau, "U.S. Census Bureau Releases New Educational Attainment Data," press release CB20-TPS.09, March 30, 2020.

6. This chapter draws on Michael Lind, "The Five Crises of the American Regime," *Tablet*, January 7, 2021.

CHAPTER ONE: THE BIG LIE

1. Quoted in Ron Suskind, *Confidence Men: Wall Street, Washington, and the Education of a President* (New York: Harper, 2011), 197.

2. For a similar argument, see Jake Rosenfeld, *You're Paid What You're Worth: And Other Myths of the Modern Economy* (Cambridge, MA: Belknap Press of Harvard University Press, 2021).

3. Academic discussions of "skill-biased technical change" include David Autor and David Dorn, "The Growth of Low-Skill Service Jobs and the Polarization of the U.S. Labor Market," *American Economic Review* 103, no. 5 (August 2013): 1553–97; David H. Autor, David Dorn, and Gordon H. Hanson, "Untangling Trade and Technology: Evidence from Local Labour Markets," *The Economic Journal* 125, no. 584 (May 2015): 621–46; David Card and John E. DiNardo, "Skill-Biased Technological Change and Rising Wage Inequality: Some Problems and Puzzles," *Journal of Labor Economics* 20, no. 4 (October 2002): 733–83; and Frank Levy and Richard J. Murnane, "U.S. Earnings Levels and Earnings Inequality: A Review of Recent Trends and Proposed Explanations," *Journal of Economic Literature* 30, no. 3 (September 1992): 1333–81.

4. James Pethokoukis, "What Progressives Get Wrong About 'Corporate Welfare,'" *The Week*, November 20, 2020.

5. Adam Smith, "On the Wages of Labour," in *An Inquiry into the Nature and Causes of the Wealth of Nations* (1776).

6. Quoted in John T. King and Mark A. Yanochik, "John Stuart Mill and the Economic Rationale for Organized Labor," *The American Economist* 56, no. 2 (2011): 28–34.

7. Quoted in Eugenio F. Biagini, "British Trade Unions and Popular Political Economy, 1860–1880," *The Historical Journal* 30, no. 4 (December 1987): 811–40.

8. Alfred Marshall, *Selected Works of Alfred Marshall for a Memorial Collection for Professor Ralph L. Dewey, 1901–1959*; A. C. Pigou, *Memorials of Alfred Marshall* (London: Macmillan and Co., 1925), 214. See also John Davidson, *The Bargain Theory of Wages* (New York: G. P. Putnam's Sons, 1898).

9. "Statistics on Union Membership," International Labor Organization, https://ilostat.ilo.org/topics/union-membership.

10. "Trade Union Density Rate, 1997 to 2021," Statistique Canada, May 30, 2022. "Trade Union Membership, UK 1995–2021," *Statistical Bulletin*, Department for Business, Energy & Industrial Strategy, May 25, 2022.

11. Florence Jaumotte and Carolina Osorio Buitron, *Inequality and Labor Market Institutions*, Staff Discussion Note SDN/15/14, International Monetary Fund, Washington, D.C., July 2015.

12. Richard B. Freeman, "How Much Has De-unionization Contributed to the Rise in Male Earnings Inequality?," in *Uneven Tides: Rising Inequality in America*, ed. Sheldon Danziger and Peter Gottschalk (New York: Russell Sage, 1994).

13. Bruce Western and Jake Rosenfeld, "Unions, Norms, and the Rise in U.S. Wage Inequality," *American Sociological Review* 75, no. 4 (August 2011).

14. Thomas Blanchet, Lucas Chancel, and Amory Gethin, "Why Is Europe More Equal Than the United States?," World Inequality Lab, November 9, 2021.

15. Anna Stansbury and Lawrence H. Summers, "The Declining Worker Power Hypothesis: An Explanation for the Recent Evolution of the American Economy," *Brookings Papers on Economic Activity* (Spring 2020): 26–27.

16. Stansbury and Summers, "Declining Worker Power Hypothesis," 21.

17. See also Kate Bahn, "'Skills Gap' Arguments Overlook Collective Bargaining and Low Minimum Wages," Washington Center for Equitable Growth, May 9, 2019.

18. Richard Barbrook and Andy Cameron, "The Californian Ideology," essay, 1995.

CHAPTER TWO: THE BAD END OF THE BARGAIN

1. Steve Jobs, remarks at Stanford University, Palo Alto, California, June 12, 2005.

2. Gerrit De Vynck, Nitasha Tiku, and Jay Greene, "Six Things to Know About the Latest Efforts to Bring Unions to Big Tech," *Washington Post*, April 30, 2021.

3. Caitlin Harrington, "The Fallout from Apple's Bizarre, Dogged Union-Busting Campaign," *Wired*, July 28, 2022.

4. Quoted in Gerrit De Vynck, Nitasha Tiku, and Jay Greene, "What You Need to Know About Unions and Big Tech," *Washington Post*, January 26, 2021.

5. U.S. Bureau of Labor Statistics, "Union Members—2021," news release, January 20, 2022.

6. U.S. Bureau of Labor Statistics, "Union Members Summary," news release, January 22, 2020.

7. John Logan, "The Union Avoidance Industry in the United States," *British Journal of Industrial Relations* 44, no. 4 (December 2006): 651–75.

8. Celine McNicholas et al., "Unlawful: U.S. Employers Are Charged with Violating Federal Law in 41.5% of All Union Election Campaigns," Economic Policy Institute, December 11, 2019.

9. A. Khalid, "Apple Hired the Same Anti-union Law Firm as Starbucks: Report," *Engadget*, April 25, 2022.

10. John Logan, "The New Union Avoidance Internationalism," *Work Organization, Labour, and Globalization* 13, no. 2 (2019).

11. Isobel Asher Hamilton, "Amazon Engaged Anti-union Consultants at a Weekly Rate of Up to $20,000 Each to Work in Its Staten Island Warehouses, Documents Suggest," *Insider*, April 20, 2022.

12. Logan, "New Union Avoidance Internationalism."

13. Tim De Chant, "Google Hired Union-Busting Consultants to Convince Employees 'Unions Suck,'" *Ars Technica*, January 11, 2022.

14. Lauren Kaori Gurley, "'Lazy,' 'Money-Oriented,' 'Single Mother': How Union-Busting Firms Compile Dossiers on Employees," *Vice*, January 5, 2021.

15. Logan, "New Union Avoidance Internationalism."

16. Logan, "New Union Avoidance Internationalism"; "Labor Board Accuses Tech Startup of Unfair Labor Practices," *Daily Labor Report*, August 30, 2018.

17. Lee Fang, "The Evolution of Union-Busting: Breaking Unions with the Language of Diversity and Social Justice," *The Intercept*, June 7, 2022.

CHAPTER THREE: BOSS RULE

1. Antitrust Guidance for Human Resource Professionals," Federal Trade Commission, Department of Justice Antitrust Division, October 2016.

2. Cassandra Carver, "How Do Anti-Trust Guidelines Impact Market Pricing?," Astron Solutions, June 25, 2019.

3. Steve Larson, "Disney, Pixar, and Lucasfilm Settle Anti-poaching Antitrust Class Action for $100 Million," Stoll Berne, February 24, 2017.

4. Gregory Wallace, "Steve Jobs Was 'Central Figure' in Silicon Valley's 'No Poaching' Case," CNN Business, August 11, 2014.

5. Sean Hollister, "Steve Jobs Personally Asked Eric Schmidt to Stop Poaching Employees, and Other Unredacted Statements in a Silicon Valley Scandal," *The Verge*, January 27, 2012.

6. Rachel Abrams, "Why Aren't Paychecks Growing? A Burger-Joint Clause Offers a Clue," *New York Times*, September 27, 2017.

7. Adam Smith, "On the Wages of Labour," in *An Inquiry into the Nature and Causes of the Wealth of Nations* (1776).

8. Evan P. Starr, J. J. Prescott, and Norman D. Bishara, "Noncompete Agreements in the U.S. Labor Force," *Journal of Law and Economics* 64, no. 1 (February 2021).

9. Peter Coy, "Why Are Fast Food Workers Signing Noncompete Agreements?," *New York Times*, September 29, 2021.

10. Susan Antilla, "Forced Arbitration Is Making It Harder for Low-Wage Workers to Seek Justice," *Capital & Main*, May 2, 2022.

11. David Weil, *The Fissured Workplace: Why Work Became So Bad for So Many and What Can Be Done to Improve It* (Cambridge, MA: Harvard University Press, 2014).

12. Adam Goldstein, "Revenge of the Managers: Labor Cost-Cutting and the Paradoxical Resurgence of Managerialism in the Shareholder Value Era, 1984 to 2001," *American Sociological Review* 77, no. 2 (April 2012): 268–94.

13. David Gordon, *Fat and Mean: The Corporate Squeeze of Working Americans and the Myth of Managerial "Downsizing"* (New York: Free Press, 1996).

CHAPTER FOUR: GLOBAL LABOR ARBITRAGE I

1. Jefferson Cowie, *Capital Moves: RCA's Seventy-Year Quest for Cheap Labor* (Ithaca, NY: Cornell University Press, 1999).

2. Alan S. Blinder, "Offshoring: Big Deal, or Business as Usual?," in *Offshoring of American Jobs: What Response from U.S. Economic Policy?*, ed. Jagdish Bhagwati and Alan S. Blinder (Cambridge, MA: MIT Press, 2009), 49, quoted in Jeff Faux, *The Servant Economy: Where America's Elite Is Sending the Middle Class* (Hoboken, NJ: John Wiley & Sons, 2012).

3. Charles A. Beard, *The Open Door at Home: A Trial Philosophy of the National Interest* (New York: Macmillan, 1935), 83.

4. Quoted in Faux, *Servant Economy*, 76.

5. Walter Wriston, *The Twilight of Sovereignty: How the Information Revolution Is Transforming Our World* (New York: Scribner, 1992), 27.

6. Quoted in "Welcome Home: The Outsourcing of Jobs to Faraway Places Is on the Wane. But This Will Not Solve the West's Employment Woes," *Economist*, January 19, 2013.

7. David H. Autor, David Dorn, and Gordon H. Hanson, "The China Shock: Learning from Labor-Market Adjustment to Large Changes in Trade," *Annual Review of Economics* 8 (2016): 205–40.

8. Susan N. Houseman, "Understanding the Decline of U.S. Manufacturing Employment" (Upjohn Institute working paper 18-287, June 1, 2018).

9. Brianna Wessling, "10 Most Automated Countries Worldwide," *The Robot Report*, December 15, 2021.

10. "South Korea: Distribution of Employment by Economic Sector from 2009 to 2019," Statista; "Distribution of the Workforce Across Economic Sectors in the United States from 2009 to 2019," Statista.

11. Paul Krugman, "In Praise of Cheap Labor: Bad Jobs at Bad Wages Are Better Than No Jobs at All," *Slate*, March 21, 1997.

12. Joe Studwell, *How Asia Works: Success and Failure in the World's Most Dynamic Region* (New York: Grove Press, 2013); Alice Amsden, *Asia's Next Giant: South Korea and Late Industrialization*, rev. ed. (Oxford: Oxford University Press, 1992); Chalmers Johnson, *MITI and the Japanese Miracle: The Growth of Indus-*

trial Policy, 1925–1975 (Stanford, CA: Stanford University Press, 1982). See also James Fallows, *Looking at the Sun: The Rise of the New East Asian Economic and Political System* (New York: Pantheon, 1994); Clyde Prestowitz, *Trading Places: How We Are Giving Our Future to Japan and How to Reclaim It* (New York: Basic Books, 1990); Richard J. Samuels, *"Rich Nation, Strong Army": National Security and the Technological Transformation of Japan* (Ithaca, NY: Cornell University Press, 1994).

13. Dwight H. Perkins and John P. Tang, "East Asian Industrial Pioneers: Japan, Korea, and Taiwan," in *The Spread of Modern Industry to the Periphery Since 1871*, ed. Kevin Hjortshøj O'Rourke and Jeffrey Gale Williamson (Oxford: Oxford University Press, 2017).

14. Wan-wen Chu, "How Taiwan Managed to Grow: Structural Transformation and Industrial Policy," in *The Oxford Handbook of Structural Transformation*, ed. Célestin Monga and Justin Yifu Lin (Oxford: Oxford University Press, 2019).

15. Jing-dong Yuan and Lorraine Eden, "Export Processing Zones in Asia: A Comparative Study," *Asian Survey* 32, no. 11 (November 1992): 1026–45.

16. "Offshoring: Is It a Win-Win Game?," McKinsey Global Institute, August 2003, 7, 9.

17. Stephen Roach, *Unbalanced: The Codependency of America and China* (New Haven, CT: Yale University Press, 2014), 35, 36.

CHAPTER FIVE: GLOBAL LABOR ARBITRAGE II

1. Vernon M. Briggs Jr., *Immigration and American Unionism* (Ithaca, NY: Cornell University Press, 2001), 170.

2. Alex Nowrasteh, Town Oh, and Artem Samiahulin, "Immigrants Reduce Unionization in the United States" (working paper no. 66, Cato Institute, June 24, 2022).

3. Harmon Leon, "Whole Foods Secretly Upgrades Tech to Target and Squash Unionizing Efforts: Data Collected by Whole Foods Suggests That Stores with Low Racial and Ethnic Diversity Are More Likely to Unionize," *Observer*, April 24, 2020.

4. James Howard Bridge, *The Inside History of the Carnegie Steel Company: A Romance of Millions* (New York: Arno Press, 1972), 81, quoted in Michael Lind, *The Next American Nation: The New Nationalism and the Fourth American Revolution* (New York: Free Press, 1995), 170–71.

5. U.S. Immigration Commission, *Abstracts of Reports of the Immigration Commission* (Washington, D.C.: U.S. Government Printing Office, 1911), quoted in David M. Gordon, Richard Edwards, and Michael Reich, *Segmented Work, Divided Workers: The Historical Transformation of Labor in the United States* (Cambridge, UK: Cambridge University Press, 1982), 141.

6. Daryl Scott, "'Immigration Indigestion': A. Philip Randolph: Radical and Restrictionist," Center for Immigration Studies, June 1, 1999.

7. Mark Hugo Lopez, Ana Gonzalez-Barrera, and Jens Manuel Krogstad, "Views of Immigration Policy," in "More Latinos Have Serious Concerns About Their Place in America Under Trump," Pew Research Center, October 25, 2018.

8. "The H-1B Visa Program and Its Impact on the U.S. Economy," Fact Sheet, American Immigration Council, July 15, 2022.

9. Julie Leininger Pycior, *LBJ & Mexican Americans: The Paradox of Power* (Austin: University of Texas Press, 1997), 75.

10. Ted Hesson, "Cesar Chavez's Complex History on Immigration," ABC News, May 1, 2013.

11. "Chavez and the UFW: A Review Essay," *Rural Migration News* 16, no. 4 (October 2010).

12. Meghan Roos and Alex J. Rouhandeh, "With Nearly Half of U.S. Farmworkers Undocumented, Ending Illegal Immigration Could Devastate Economy," *Newsweek*, April 21, 2021.

13. Giovanni Peri, "How Immigrants Affect California Employment and Wages," *California Counts: Population Trends and Profiles* 8, no. 3 (February 2007): 1.

14. "Illegal Aliens: Influence of Illegal Workers on Wages and Working Conditions of Legal Workers," *Briefing Report to Congressional Requesters*, B-222748, General Accounting Office, Washington, D.C., March 10, 1988.

15. "Illegal Aliens," 33–34.

16. "Illegal Aliens," 35–36.

17. "Illegal Aliens," 37.

18. "Illegal Aliens," 38.

19. "Illegal Aliens," 39.

20. Natalie Kitroeff, "Immigrants Flooded California. Construction Worker Pay Sank. Here's Why," *Los Angeles Times*, April 22, 2017.

21. Sara Murray, "On the Killing Floor, Clues to the Impact of Immigration on Jobs," *Wall Street Journal*, August 21, 2013.

22. "Characteristics of H-1B Specialty Occupation Workers," Fiscal Year 2021 Annual Report to Congress, October 1, 2020—September 30, 2021, U.S. Citizenship and Immigration Services, U.S. Department of Homeland Security, March 2, 2022.

23. Norman Matloff, "H-1Bs: Still Not the Best and Brightest," Center for Immigration Studies, Backgrounder, May 2008.

24. Julia Preston, "Pink Slips at Disney. But First, Training Foreign Replacements," *New York Times*, June 3, 2015. See also Stef W. Kight, "U.S. Companies Are Forcing Workers to Train Their Own Foreign Replacements," *Axios*, December 29, 2019; Patrick Thibodeau, "This IT Worker Had to Train an H-1B Replacement," *Computerworld*, June 10, 2014; "Untold Stories: The American Workers Replaced by the H-1B Visa Program," Center for Immigration Studies, May 4, 2019.

25. Daniel Costa and Ron Hira, "H-1B Visas and Prevailing Wage Levels," Economic Policy Institute, May 4, 2020.

26. "3.4 Poverty and Welfare Utilization," in *The Economic and Fiscal Consequences of Immigration* (Washington, D.C.: National Academies Press, 2017).

27. Miriam Valverde, "Perdue Cites Data on Immigrant Households Benefiting from Social Welfare Programs," PolitiFact, August 14, 2017.

28. "Immigrant Share of the U.S. Population and Civilian Labor Force, 1980–Present," Migration Policy Institute.

29. "International Migration 2020 Highlights," Department of Economic and Social Affairs, United Nations.

30. "Remittances, Percent of GDP," Country Rankings, TheGlobalEconomy
.com; Dilip Ratha, "What Are Remittances," International Monetary
Fund.

31. Jeffrey S. Passel and D'Vera Cohn, "Industries of Unauthorized Immigrant Workers," in "Share of Unauthorized Immigrant Workers in Production, Construction Jobs Falls Since 2007," Pew Research Center, March 26,
2015.

32. Jens Manuel Krogstad, Mark Hugo Lopez, and Jeffrey S. Passel, "A Majority of Americans Say Immigrants Mostly Fill Jobs U.S. Citizens Do Not
Want," Pew Research Center, June 10, 2020.

33. National Research Council, *The New Americans: Economic, Demographic, and
Fiscal Effects of Immigration*, ed. James P. Smith and Barry Edmonston (Washington, D.C.: National Academy Press, 1997), 236, cited in Briggs, *Immigration and American Unionism*, 153.

34. National Research Council, *The New Americans*.

CHAPTER SIX: SCROOGE REVISITED

1. Adam Smith, "On the Wages of Labour," in *An Inquiry into the Nature and
Causes of the Wealth of Nations* (1776).

2. Smith, "On the Wages of Labour."

3. Smith, "On the Wages of Labour."

4. Adam Smith, "On Wages and Profits in the Different Employments of Labour and Stock," in *An Inquiry into the Nature and Causes of the Wealth of Nations*
(1776).

5. Charles Dickens, *A Christmas Carol* (New York: Bantam Classics, 1986).

6. Tracey A. Loveless, "Most Families That Received SNAP Benefits in 2018
Had at Least One Person Working," U.S. Census, July 21, 2020.

7. "Millions of Full-Time U.S. Workers Receive Federal Health Care and
Food Assistance," CBS News, November 20, 2020.

8. Clare O'Connor, "Reports: Fast Food Companies Outsource $7 Billion in
Annual Labor Costs to Taxpayers," *Forbes*, October 16, 2013.

9. Clare O'Connor, "Report: Walmart Cost Taxpayers $6.2 Billion in Public Assistance," *Forbes*, April 24, 2014.

10. "Super-Sizing Public Costs: How Low Wages at Top Fast-Food Chains Leave Taxpayers Footing the Bill," National Employment Law Project, October 15, 2013.

11. Ken Jacobs, Ian Eve Perry, and Jenifer MacGillvary, "The High Public Cost of Low Wages," UC Berkeley Labor Center, April 13, 2015.

12. Russell Sykes, "Making Work Pay in New York," Empire Center, April 18, 2012.

13. Jacob S. Hacker, *The Great Risk Shift: The New Economic Insecurity and the Decline of the American Dream* (Oxford: Oxford University Press, 2006).

14. "Policy Basics: The Earned Income Tax Credit," Center on Budget and Policy Priorities, updated December 10, 2019.

15. Teresa Ghilarducci and Aida Farmand, "What's Not to Like About the EITC? Plenty, It Turns Out," *American Prospect*, June 28, 2019.

16. Walter Korpi, "Faces of Inequality: Gender, Class, and Patterns of Inequalities in Different Types of Welfare States," *Social Politics: International Studies in Gender, State, and Society* 7, no. 2 (Summer 2000): 127–91.

17. Juliana Menasce Horowitz, "Despite Challenges at Home and Work, Most Working Moms and Dads Say Being Employed Is What's Best for Them," Pew Research Center, September 12, 2019.

18. Megan Brenan, "Record-High 56% of U.S. Women Prefer Working to Homemaking," Gallup, October 24, 2019.

19. Juliana Menasce Horowitz, "Despite Challenges at Home and Work."

20. Wells King, "Let Them Eat Daycare," American Compass, March 1, 2021.

21. "Op-Ed by Commerce Secretary Gina Raimondo: A Tattered Care Economy Is Holding Back American Workers," U.S. Department of Commerce, Office of Public Affairs, July 20, 2021.

22. "Fact Sheet: The American Families Plan," White House, April 28, 2021.

23. Ann Shola Orloff, "Farewell to Maternalism? State Policies and Mothers'

Employment" (working paper, Institute for Policy Research Northwestern University Working Paper Series).

CHAPTER SEVEN: THE CREDENTIAL ARMS RACE

1. Oren Cass, "The Cost of Thriving," *American Affairs* 4, no. 1 (Spring 2020): 15–32.

2. Aimee Picchi, "It Now Takes Up to 66 Weeks to Pay for 52 Weeks of Middle-Class Basics," MoneyWatch, CBS News, February 27, 2020.

3. "Educational Attainment Distribution in the United States from 1960 to 2021," Statista, June 10, 2022.

4. Lawrence Mishel, Lynn Rhinehart, and Lane Windham, "Explaining the Erosion of Private-Sector Unions: How Corporate Practices and Legal Changes Have Undercut the Ability of Workers to Organize and Bargain," Economic Policy Institute, November 18, 2020.

5. Council of Economic Advisers, "Occupational Licensing: A Framework for Policymakers," Council of Economic Advisers Report, July 2015, 3.

6. Rob Valletta, "Higher Education, Wages, and Polarization," *RBSF Economic Letter* 2015-02, January 12, 2015.

7. Morris M. Kleiner and Alan B. Krueger, "The Prevalence and Effects of Occupational Licensing," *British Journal of Industrial Relations* 48 (2010): 676–87.

8. "Unions Help Reduce Disparities and Strengthen Our Democracy," Fact Sheet, Economic Policy Institute, April 23, 2021.

9. Morris M. Kleiner and Alan B. Krueger, "Analyzing the Extent and Influence of Occupational Licensing on the Labor Market" (IZA discussion paper no. 5505, February 2011), 24.

10. Catherine Thorbecke, "Amazon Raising Hourly Pay for Warehouse and Delivery Workers," CNN Business, September 29, 2022.

11. Brink Lindsey and Steven M. Teles, *The Captured Economy: How the Powerful Enrich Themselves, Slow Down Growth, and Increase Inequality* (Oxford: Oxford University Press, 2017).

12. "Undergraduate Enrollment," National Center for Education Statistics, last updated May 2021.

13. Mark J. Perry, "Diversity and Administrative Bloat in Higher Education," AEI, July 24, 2018.

14. *Griggs v. Duke Power Co.*, 401 U.S. 424 (1971).

CHAPTER EIGHT: CASCADE EFFECT

1. Christopher A. Julian, "Median Age at First Marriage, 2021," National Center for Family & Marriage Research, Bowling Green State University.

2. W. Bradford Wilcox and Wendy Wang, "The Marriage Divide: How and Why Working-Class Families Are More Fragile Today," Institute for Family Studies, September 25, 2017.

3. Kim Parker and Renee Stepler, "As U.S. Marriage Rate Hovers at 50%, Education Gap in Marital Status Widens," Pew Research Center, September 14, 2017.

4. Maarten J. Bijlsma and Ben Wilson, "Modelling the Socio-economic Determinants of Fertility: A Mediation Analysis Using the Parametric G-Formula," *Journal of the Royal Statistical Society: Series A* (Statistics in Society) 183, no. 2 (2020): 493–513.

5. Anne Case and Angus Deaton, *Deaths of Despair and the Future of Capitalism* (Princeton, NJ: Princeton University Press, 2020).

6. William Julius Wilson, *When Work Disappears: The World of the New Urban Poor* (New York: Knopf, 1996).

7. Theda Skocpol, *Diminished Democracy* (Norman: University of Oklahoma Press, 2004).

8. Robert Putnam, *Bowling Alone: The Collapse and Revival of American Community* (New York: Simon & Schuster, 2000).

9. Daniel A. Cox, "Men's Social Circles Are Shrinking," Survey Center on American Life, AEI, June 29, 2021.

10. Zach Goldberg, "America's White Saviors," *Tablet,* June 5, 2019.

11. Peter Turchin, "Blame Rich, Overeducated Elites as Society Frays," Bloomberg, November 12, 2016.

12. Kayla Rodgers, "Student Gets into Stanford after Writing #BlackLivesMatter on Application 100 Times," CNN, April 5, 2017.

13. Elizabeth Redden, "41% of Recent Grads Work in Jobs Not Requiring a Degree," *Inside Higher Ed*, February 18, 2020.

14. "The Permanent Detour: Underemployment's Long-Term Effects on the Careers of College Grads," Burning Glass, May 2018.

15. John Chamberlain, *The American Stakes* (New York: Carrick & Evans, 1940).

16. See generally Michael Lind, *The New Class War: Saving Democracy from the Managerial Elite* (New York: Portfolio, 2020).

17. "National Primary Turnout Hits New Record Low," Governance Program, Democracy Project, Bipartisan Policy Center, October 2012.

18. Elaine Kamarck and Alexander R. Podkul, "The 2018 Primaries Project: The Demographics of Primary Voters," Brookings Institution, October 23, 2018.

19. Martin Gilens and Benjamin I. Page, "Testing Theories of American Politics: Elites, Interest Groups, and Average Citizens," *Perspectives on Politics* 12, no. 3 (2014): 564–81. See also Martin Gilens and Benjamin I. Page, *Democracy in America? What Has Gone Wrong and What We Can Do About It* (Chicago: University of Chicago Press, 2017); Martin Gilens and Benjamin I. Page, "Critics Argued with Our Analysis of US Political Inequality. Here Are 5 Ways They're Wrong," *The Monkey Cage* (blog), *Washington Post*, May 23, 2016.

20. Megan Brenan, "Approval of Labor Unions at Highest Point Since 1965," Gallup, September 2, 2021.

21. Kim Parker and Kiley Hurst, "Growing Share of Americans Say They Want More Spending on Police in Their Area," Pew Research Center, October 26, 2021.

22. Nikki Graf, "Most Americans Say Colleges Should Not Consider Race or Ethnicity in Admissions," Pew Research Center, February 25, 2019.

23. Michael Lind, "Hub City Riot Ninjas," *Tablet*, June 2, 2020.

CHAPTER NINE: THE MYTHS OF NEOLIBERAL GLOBALIZATION

1. Erika Na, "China's Shipbuilding Progress Threatens South Korea's Long-Held Tech Dominance in the Industry," *South China Morning Post*, September 23, 2022.

2. Gina Chon, "DJI Is a More Elusive U.S. Target Than Huawei," *Reuters*, December 16, 2021.

3. Stephen Ezell, "Going, Going, Gone? To Stay Competitive in Biopharmaceuticals, America Must Learn from Its Semiconductor Mistakes," Information Technology and Innovation Foundation, November 22, 2021.

4. "China's Wind Giant Sees Demand Boom Resuming After 2021 Blip," *Bloomberg News*, October 27, 2021.

5. "GWEC Releases Supply Side Data 2018 Report," Windfair, April 17, 2019.

6. Lili Pike, "China Is Owning the Global Battery Race. That Could Be a Problem for the U.S.," *Grid*, December 28, 2021, updated January 18, 2022.

7. Yanzhong Huang, "The Coronavirus Outbreak Could Disrupt the U.S. Drug Supply," Council on Foreign Relations, March 5, 2020.

8. Dillon Jaghory, "Japan's Robot Dominance," Nasdaq, May 16, 2022.

9. Quoted in Nikil Saval, "Globalisation: The Rise and Fall of an Idea That Swept the World," *Guardian*, July 14, 2017.

10. Robert L. Bartley, "Open Nafta Borders? Why Not?," *Wall Street Journal*, July 2, 2001.

11. Quoted in Saval, "Globalisation."

12. "Wrong All Along," American Compass, March 17, 2022.

13. Ryan Bourne, "Tony Blair Is Right: Globalisation Is a Fact Not a Choice," Cato Institute, March 1, 2019.

14. Testimony of Lawrence Summers To House Panel on U.S.-China Trade, *Wall Street Journal*, May 4, 2000.

15. John Maynard Keynes, "National Self-Sufficiency," *Yale Review* 22, no. 4 (June 1933).

16. Nicholas Kaldor, "The Foundations of Free Trade Theory and Their Implications for the Current World Recession," in *Unemployment in Western Countries*, ed. Edmond Malinvaud and Jean-Paul Fitoussi (London: Palgrave Macmillan, 1980).

17. Ralph E. Gomory and William J. Baumol, *Global Trade and Conflicting National Interests* (Cambridge, MA: MIT Press, 2000).

18. Paul A. Samuelson, "Where Ricardo and Mill Rebut and Confirm Arguments of Mainstream Economists Supporting Globalization," *Journal of Economic Perspectives* 18 (Summer 2004); "Response from Paul A. Samuelson," *Journal of Economic Perspectives* 19 (Summer 2005).

19. Paul R. Krugman, "Is Free Trade Passé?," *Journal of Economic Perspectives* 1, no. 2 (Fall 1987): 131–44.

20. Michael Lind, "The Strange Career of Paul Krugman," *Tablet*, November 22, 2021.

21. Steven Pearlstein, "Trading Shots with a Wunderkind," *Washington Post*, April 3, 1994.

22. Paul Krugman, "What Economists (Including Me) Got Wrong About Globalization," *Bloomberg*, October 10, 2019.

23. Stephen Roach, *Unbalanced: The Codependency of America and China* (New Haven, CT: Yale University Press, 2014), 142.

CHAPTER TEN: BEYOND GLOBAL ARBITRAGE

1. Abraham Lincoln, "I Am Humble Abraham Lincoln," in Marion Mills Miller, ed., *Life and Works of Abraham Lincoln*, vol. 3.

2. Michael Lind, *Land of Promise: An Economic History of the United States* (New York: HarperCollins, 2012).

3. For the tradition of American developmentalism, see Lind, *Land of Promise*; and Michael Lind, ed., *Hamilton's Republic: Readings in the American Democratic Nationalist Tradition* (New York: Free Press, 1997). See also Erik Reinert, *How Rich Countries Got Rich and Why Poor Countries Stay Poor* (New York: Carroll & Graf, 2007); Erik Reinert, *The Visionary Realism of German Economics from the Thirty Years' War to the Cold War* (London: Anthem Press, 2019); Ha-

Joon Chang, *Kicking Away the Ladder: Developmental Strategy in Historical Perspective* (London: Anthem Press, 2002); Paul Bairoch, *Economics and World History: Myths and Paradoxes* (Chicago: University of Chicago Press, 1993); James Fallows, *Looking at the Sun: The Rise of the New East Asian Economic and Political System* (New York: Pantheon, 1994); Joe Studwell, *How Asia Works: Success and Failure in the World's Most Dynamic Region* (New York: Grove Press, 2013); Clyde Prestowitz, *The Betrayal of American Prosperity: Free Market Delusions, America's Decline, and How We Must Compete in the Post-Dollar Era* (New York: Free Press, 2010); Robert D. Atkinson, *The Past and Future of America's Economy: Long Waves of Innovation That Power Cycles of Growth* (Cheltenham, UK: Edward Elgar, 2005).

4. Robert D. Atkinson and Michael Lind, "Small Business Boards: A Proposal to Raise Productivity and Wages in All 50 States and the District of Columbia," Information Technology and Innovation Foundation, April 5, 2021.

5. Robert Fogel, "Forecasting the Cost of U.S. Health Care," September 3, 2009. See also William J. Baumol et al., *The Cost Disease: Why Computers Get Cheaper and Health Care Doesn't* (New Haven, CT: Yale University Press, 2012).

6. Frank J. Lysy, "Productivity: Do Low Real Wages Explain the Slowdown?," *An Economic Sense* (blog), n.d.

7. Maria Sachetti, "Florida Needs Workers to Rebuild After Ian. Undocumented Immigrants Are Stepping In," *Washington Post*, October 23, 2022.

8. Paul Mason, "Our Problem Isn't Robots, It's the Low-Wage Car-Wash Economy," *Guardian*, December 12, 2016.

9. John Hicks, *The Theory of Wages* (London: Macmillan, 1932).

10. H. J. Habakkuk, *American and British Technology in the Nineteenth Century: The Search for Labour-Saving Inventions* (London: Cambridge University Press, 1962).

11. Michael A. Clemens, Ethan G. Lewis, and Hannah M. Postel, "Immigration Restrictions as Active Labor Market Policy: Evidence from the Mexican Bracero Exclusion," *American Economic Review* 108, no. 6 (June 2018): 1468–87.

12. Bob Davis, "The Thorny Economics of Illegal Immigration: Arizona's

Economy Took a Hit When Many Illegal Immigrants Left, but Benefits Also Materialized," *Wall Street Journal*, February 9, 2016.

13. Harry J. Holzer, "Tight Labor Markets and Wage Growth in the Current Economy," Brookings, April 13, 2022.

14. Rhonda Fanning, "What Barbara Jordan & Current GOP Rhetoric Have in Common," *Texas Standard: The National Daily News Show of Texas*, February 19, 2016.

CHAPTER ELEVEN: HOW TO RESTORE WORKER POWER IN AMERICA

1. Quoted in Winifred D. Wandersee, "'I'd Rather Pass a Law Than Organize a Union': Frances Perkins and the Reformist Approach to Organized Labor," *Labor History* 34, no. 1 (1993): 5–32.

2. "Samuel Gompers," Labor History, AFL-CIO.

3. Samuel Gompers, "To Affiliated Unions," *National Labor Standard*, July 1896.

4. Sharon Block and Benjamin Sacks, *Clean Slate for Worker Power: Building a Just Economy and Democracy*, Clean Slate for Worker Power, Harvard Law School, January 23, 2020.

5. Liz Shuler (@LizSchuler), "Access to health care without fear and intimidation is every person's right. We must be able to control our own bodies—which has a direct impact on economic justice and the ability of working people to make a better life for themselves and their families," Twitter, May 3, 2022.

6. "Not What They Bargained For: A Survey of American Workers," American Compass, September 6, 2021.

7. Ben Zipperer, "Gradually Raising the Minimum Wage to $15 Would Be Good for Workers, Good for Businesses, and Good for the Economy," testimony before the U.S. House of Representatives Committee on Education and Labor, February 7, 2019, Economic Policy Institute.

8. Nicolas Vega, "After Inflation, People Making U.S. Minimum Wage Are Earning Less Now Than 60 Years Ago," CNBC, July 20, 2022.

9. Amina Dunn, "Most Americans Support a $15 Federal Minimum Wage," Pew Research Center, April 22, 2021.

10. "Living Wage Calculator," Massachusetts Institute of Technology, accessed July 13, 2002.

11. James K. Galbraith, Michael Lind, and Martin J. Luby, "The Case for Revenue Sharing: Fiscal Equalization and the COVID-19 Recession," University of Texas at Austin, Lyndon B. Johnson School of Public Affairs, December 8, 2020.

12. "Who Are the Parties? Thirty Seven Railroads and Twelve Unions," National Railway Labor Conference.

13. "Transportation and Warehousing: NAICS 48-49," Industries at a Glance, U.S. Bureau of Labor Statistics.

14. Winston Churchill, speech, Trade Boards Bill, H.C. Deb. April 28, 1909, vol. 4, cols. 342–411.

15. Donald Hirsch, "How the Old Idea of the Living Wage Has Been Adopted by the Political Establishment," *The Conversation*, June 6, 2017.

16. Kate Andrias, "An American Approach to Social Democracy: The Forgotten Promise of the Fair Labor Standards Act," *Yale Law Journal* 128, no. 3 (January 2019).

17. Kate Andrias, "Social Bargaining in States and Cities: Toward a More Egalitarian and Democratic Workplace Law" (paper, Harvard Law Reform Symposium, September 19, 2017), 6nn33, 32.

18. Mike Vilensky, "New York Wage Boards Shaped Policy for Decades," *Wall Street Journal*, August 6, 2015; Amy Traub, "The NY Wage Board Delivers for Fast Food Workers," *Demos*, July 22, 2015; Joshua Solomon, "State Wage Board Recommends 40-Hour Work Week for Farm Laborers," *Times Union*, September 6, 2022.

19. New York Senate Bill S6578, www.nysenate.gov/legislation/bills/2019/s6578.

20. Robert D. Atkinson and Michael Lind, "Small Business Boards: A Proposal to Raise Productivity and Wages in All 50 States and the District of Columbia," Information Technology and Innovation Foundation, April 5, 2021.

CHAPTER TWELVE: "KEEP YOUR GOVERNMENT HANDS OFF MY MEDICARE"

1. This chapter draws on Michael Lind, "The Government Should Keep Its Hands Off Your Medicare: On Contributory Social Insurance and the Work Ethic," American Compass, October 15, 2021.

2. Philip Rucker, "Sen. DeMint of S.C. Is Voice of Opposition to Health-Care Reform," *Washington Post*, July 28, 2009.

3. Tyler Cowen, "The Funniest Sentence I Read Today," *Marginal Revolution*, July 27, 2009.

4. Timothy Noah, "The Medicare-Isn't-Government Meme," *Slate*, August 5, 2009.

5. Franklin D. Roosevelt, State of the Union address, 1935.

6. Quoted in "Luther Gulick Memorandum re: Famous FDR Quote," Research Notes and Special Studies by the Historian's Office, Social Security Administration.

7. "Taxing Wages—the United States," OECD, 2022.

8. Juliette Cubanski, Tricia Neuman, and Meredith Freed, "Sources of Medicaid Revenue, 2018," in "The Facts on Medicare Spending and Financing," KFF, August 20, 2019.

AFTERWORD: MAKING AMERICA WORK FOR AMERICAN WORKERS

1. Megan Brenan, "Approval of Labor Unions at Highest Point Since 1965," Gallup, September 2, 2021.

2. Kim Parker, Rich Morin, and Juliana Menasce Horowitz, "Retirement, Social Security, and Long-Term Care," in "Looking to the Future, Public Sees an America in Decline on Many Fronts," Pew Research Center, March 21, 2019.

3. Jeffrey E. Cohen, *Presidential Responsiveness and Public Policy-Making: The Public and the Policies That Presidents Choose* (Ann Arbor: University of Michigan Press, 1997).

4. Scott Clement and Dan Balz, "Americans Sense China Eclipsing U.S. Economically and Say Protecting U.S. Jobs Should Be Priority, Poll Finds," *Washington Post*, October 7, 2021.

5. John Halpin et al., "America Adrift: How the U.S. Foreign Policy Debate Misses What Voters Really Want," Center for American Progress, May 5, 2019.

6. "Gallup Historical Trends: Immigration," Gallup, news.gallup.com/poll/1660/immigration.aspx.

7. Michael Lind, *The New Class War: Saving Democracy from the Managerial Elite* (New York: Portfolio, 2020). See also Joel Kotkin, *The Coming of Neo-feudalism: A Warning to the Global Middle Class* (New York: Encounter Books, 2020).